T0324282

"*Organic Ministry to Women* should be requi[red] ... ministry to women in a church, campus, or mission context! Edwards and Mathews include solid, biblical support; insightful history on how ministry to women has gotten to where it is today; and very practical methodology. This is a robust organizational and leadership resource. If you are eager for effective ministry training, this book delivers essential guidance, direction, and wisdom."

—Dr. Pamela MacRae
Professor of ministry to women, Moody Bible Institute

"I am a retired pastor of women with a longing heart to see women grow and thrive. Most ministry books identify the challenge and peel back the layers of that challenge. *Organic Ministry to Women: A Guide to Transformational Ministry with Next Generation Women* goes beyond and actually explains how to meet that challenge and develop a ministry that will grow each woman, and all women, into what God desires them to be. Paul advised Titus to find women who would share their lives and set an example. And here in the twenty-first century we are to do the same: Allow women to "pass through our hands and hearts" and emerge to do the same for others. I highly recommend *Organic Ministry to Women*. Don't wait—get your copy now—it will transform your ministry and your life."

—Dr. Cynthia Fantasia
Former pastor to women at Grace Chapel, Lexington, MA
Author of *In the Lingering Light: Courage and Hope for the Alzheimer's Caregiver*

"As a mentor of young women both in the corporate world and the church, I've discipled women in a variety of settings—the local coffee shop, the boardroom, my kitchen table, via video chat, and the typical Sunday school classroom. Except for the latter, how I minister looks nothing like how my grandmother did women's ministry. The postmodern woman no longer fits into a simple, neat box. She juggles more than her predecessors and craves, even demands, authenticity. *Organic Ministry to Women* is a much-needed resource helping pastoral leaders transform their methods of discipleship from the ways of their youth to what's relevant and needed for women today. When we, as pastoral leaders, realize we need to do the changing, we adopt the same attitude as the apostle Paul, 'I try to find common ground with everyone, doing everything I can to save some' (1 Cor. 9:22, NLT)."

—Karla D. Zazueta
Architect turned discipleship leader and blogger
Author of *Discipleship for Hispanic Introverts*
Contributing author to *Vindicating the Vixens*

"Ministry leaders eager to see the transformational power of Christ in the women they lead need this resource. *Organic Ministry to Women* is relevant and practical—creating the perfect balance of inspiration and how-tos."

—Kat Armstrong,
Executive director of Polished Ministries (www.polishedonline.org)
Author of *No More Holding Back*

"This is such a needed resource for anyone involved in ministering to women! *Organic Ministry to Women* reminds us that the church is a unique sphere where women from Gen Z to the Greatest Generation engage. This book serves as a step-by-step instruction guide to unite women across ages and stages, especially as we work to include them all in our ministry. Through the Transformation Model, Sue Edwards and Kelley Mathews empower us to focus on Bible study and prayer as the bedrock of ministry. At the same time, they encourage us to seek new ways to engage women in our congregations. If our churches can inspire women to live out Titus 2:3–5, as Edwards and Mathews describe, a watching world will be drawn to the Jesus we love and serve."

—Angela Cirocco
Minister to women, Northwest Bible Church, Dallas, TX

"A lot has changed over the past seventeen years since Sue Edwards and Kelley Mathews wrote their first book about ministry with women. *Organic Ministry to Women* addresses many of these changes in order to more effectively reach out and care for women in the twenty-first-century church, campus, and mission field. The book gives excellent insights into different generations and offers practical ways to bring together women of all ages. The distinctives of large and small churches make the book applicable for any size women's ministry, and the profiles of different women emphasize that God uses all types of women to impact the world for Jesus Christ. Read this book and you, too, will be better equipped to make a difference in the lives of women."

—Dr. Joye Baker
Adjunct professor of educational ministries and leadership, Dallas Theological Seminary

"Many women in the workplace today are frustrated with the reception they receive from leaders in 'the church' when God has gifted them with gifts of leadership. *Organic Ministry to Women: A Guide to Transformational Ministry with Next Generation Women* provides a wonderful Christlike mindset and roadmap for navigating these landmines, resulting in many people being introduced to Jesus through them as they follow God's calling on their lives. While very practical, humorous stories inject vivid pictures as God helps these women's ministry leaders through unexpected circumstances."

—Diane Paddison
Founder and executive director, www.4wordwomen.org,
Author of *Work, Love, Pray* and *Be Refreshed: A Year of Devotions for Women in the Workplace*

Organic
MINISTRY
to Women

A Guide to Transformational Ministry
with Next Generation Women

SUE EDWARDS & KELLEY MATHEWS

Organic Ministry to Women: A Guide to Transformational Ministry with Next Generation Women

© 2019 by Sue Edwards and Kelley Mathews

Published by Kregel Ministry, an imprint of Kregel Publications, 2450 Oak Industrial Dr. NE, Grand Rapids, MI 49505-6020.

Scripture quotations are from the Holy Bible, New International Version®, NIV®. Copyright © 1973, 1978, 1984, 2011 by Biblica, Inc.™ Used by permission of Zondervan. All rights reserved worldwide. www.zondervan.com

The Greek font, GraecaU, is available from www.linguistsoftware.com/lgku.htm, +1-425-775-1130.

Sample Bible Study in Appendix B taken from *James: Discovering God's Delight in a Lived-Out Faith*, The Discover Together Bible Study Series, by Sue Edwards, 2019, Kregel Publications (https://www.discovertogetherseries.com).

ISBN 978-0-8254-4615-3

Printed in the United States of America

19 20 21 22 23 / 5 4 3 2 1

To Natalie Edwards, Lindsay Ann Nickens, and Amanda Sherzer, who inspire in us great hope and confidence in the younger generation rising to take the reins of leadership with "integrity of heart" and "skillful hands" (Psalm 78:72).

CONTENTS

FOREWORD

Women's ministry in our local churches is changing. Since we wrote the first edition in 2002, new generations have stepped into shared leadership with older generations. This update will assist the church to be even more relevant and fruitful in ministry to women today.
—Sue and Kelley

I have had the incredible honor of serving alongside Dr. Sue Edwards for many years as colleagues at Dallas Theological Seminary and colaborers for the cause of Christ. Sue is a respected member of the seminary teaching faculty, who is loved by her coworkers and more importantly by her students. She is truly a masterful teacher and communicator in the classroom, who earns the respect of her students. Through her years of service at the seminary and in local churches, Sue has had the fantastic opportunity to influence an entire new generation of women leaders for the worldwide church. This book is one of the tools of that influence. The global church is richer because of Sue's impact.

One of those former students Sue influenced is Kelley Mathews, whom I have also known for many years. An excellent author and wordsmith in her own right, Kelley has helped others to fulfill their own dream of entering the publishing world by offering her editorial skills and guidance. Sue would be the first to tell you that she is a stronger writer because of Kelley's influence. Kelley continues to write actively to address the needs of her readers through her work with books, magazines, and blogs.

So putting these two women together on a book project like this is exciting. But why is a second edition needed? With this second edition, both Sue and Kelley are able to expand and explore the world women find themselves in today. A lot has changed in a very short time since the first edition came out. In our age of social media awareness campaigns, women's issues dominate many political discussions while churches and ministries are stumbling to address ethical crises in biblical and respectful ways. Local churches and parachurch ministries cannot afford to ignore our ministry to women and with women. More than ever, churches and ministries need equipped godly women not on the sidelines but on the front lines.

Christian organizations are only truly healthy when both men and women have opportunities to learn, grow, and serve together. Ministering to the women in our midst is not a "fluffy luxury" for only the privileged few, or a "second-class" afterthought on the activities calendar. Healthy, biblical ministries to women and with women are foundational to the work of the gospel. My prayer is that this book will help to equip Christian leaders like yourself in leading life-changing ministry that is both relevant and biblically grounded. We cannot afford half-hearted effort or allow any of our women to fall through the cracks. The work is just too important.

And now, a word to my brothers in Christ: If you are picking up this book, good for you! The secular, unbelieving world watches how we treat our sisters in Christ. One of the greatest witnesses we have as believers is the love and respect we show one another. So to you who serve in leadership roles in local churches and parachurch ministries, make it a priority to give the women leaders in your midst the resources, respect, and support they need. Reading this book is a great first step to understanding the needs of women in your church or ministry settings.

—Dr. George M. Hillman Jr.,
vice president of student life, dean of students,
professor of educational ministries and leadership,
Dallas Theological Seminary

While various forms of women's ministry have existed for decades, especially in denominational churches, fewer of the present forms effectively reach the next generation because they appear irrelevant to the issues and needs of women today. To reach a new generation we, with a heart for women, must be open to change, flexing in our methods while firmly holding to the center, the Word of God.

This book contains a concise and clear explanation of the differences between the modern and the postmodern women of our culture. It also introduces the Transformation Model, which addresses and adapts to the needs of the postmodern woman, as a solution. However, Sue and Kelley maintain a fine balance between the necessity to minister to the needs of young women while not neglecting the valuable resource found in older women. These experienced, mature women must be encouraged to obey the Titus 2:3–5 command to be the mentors and role models for the generations following them.

The importance of their emphasis that the teaching of Scripture must be the core focus of any ministry cannot be overestimated. Without consistent Bible teaching with application to women's lives, spiritual growth will not be constant. Every other activity finds its source in this focus. Consequently, the relationships that develop among women are not shallow and superficial, but are genuinely caring and nurturing.

Since Sue ministered in a large church and Kelley in a small one, they offer valuable insights on how these new methods can be adapted to churches of any size. They are practical and honest in describing their own experiences and the methods and activities they've tried. Some were successful; some were not. This knowledge gives the book credibility you can trust. It has been forged from years of experience.

The scope of the book is not limited to the local church. Ideas on starting ministries on college campuses, both Christian and secular, are given. An excellent chapter on using the model cross-culturally will be very useful in creatively planning a missions outreach.

This book is a valuable resource for anyone involved in women's ministries, whether it's a church, campus, or missions program, and even for those ministering one-on-one. I'm happy to recommend it as an essential ministry tool for communicating the Word of God and building life-sustaining relationships.

—Vickie Kraft
minister to women, Northwest Bible Church (1985–1998)

ACKNOWLEDGMENTS

There is a sense in which no gift is ours until we have thanked the giver. Thank you, Lord Jesus, for you are the greatest Giver of all.

Sue Edwards:

To David, my husband of forty-eight years, *"the wind beneath my wings."* Without your encouragement, flexibility, unselfishness, and expertise with the computer, this book would not exist. To our daughters Heather and Rachel, for lighting our world as we watched you grow into beautiful women inside and out. To Tom and Matt, for loving them the way we do and for being God's men. And thanks for a new generation of joy, grandchildren Becca, Luke, Caleb, Will, and Seth. And finally, to my grandmother who gave me my first glimpse of God.

Thanks, Kelley, for sharing your writing skills, your fine mind, and your heart for women on this project. God brought us together and I could not have orchestrated a better team. Your flexibility and maturity beyond your years made working with you a joy every step of the way. And thanks for the computer shortcuts you taught me. You can teach an old dog new tricks!

Kelley Mathews:

To the women whom God has used to mold my character and faith, and to the women who have found this book useful for ministry over the years: Thank you for investing in and participating with me as we have served God. My deepest thanks to Sue for partnering so generously for more than a decade; to Sandra Glahn for training, mentoring, and cheering me on; and to my family for supporting my writing career in all its ups and downs.

A hearty thanks from both of us to Natalie Edwards (no relation to Sue), Lindsay Ann Nickens, and Amanda Sherzer for their insight and contributions interviewing and writing the "Women of Influence" profiles.

Information about the authors:

SUE EDWARDS (DMIN, GORDON-CONWELL) spent several decades overseeing women's ministries in large evangelical churches. Today she joyfully invests in men and women at Dallas Theological Seminary (DTS) as professor of educational ministries and leadership. She loves writing Bible studies and teaching the Bible. The author of The Discover Together Bible Study series (discovertogetherseries.com), she has been married to David for over forty-eight years and they are the parents of two daughters, Heather and Rachel, and grandparents to five. She and David live in the Dallas area with their two Westies, Quigley and Emma Jane.

Sue is a founding member of the Association of Women in Ministry Professions, an organization that promotes personal and professional growth in their members, all serving as women's ministry directors, pastors, consultants, educators, writers, and trainers. For information on AWMP, visit www.awmp.org.

KELLEY MATHEWS (THM, DALLAS SEMINARY) wrote the first version of this book as a new mother. Now, she and her husband of twenty-plus years have three sons and a daughter.

When the kids were small, she spent several years leading a small church women's ministry. She currently writes and edits in the Christian book market, also judging fiction for the Christy Awards and writing reviews for *Publishers Weekly*. Although she and Sue enjoy different life stages, they share the same passion: to see women won, grown, and unleashed for God's glory. They bring different perspectives that benefit a variety of readers.

INTRODUCTION

Women's gatherings feel cheesy—like a big flashy production. They don't draw us closer to Jesus or each other. Honestly, I think that's why most women my age aren't coming anymore. Can we try something different? My friends and I have some fresh ideas.

Ministry to women is changing. We hear these kinds of comments from women in their twenties, thirties, and even forties, as they partner with older women in churches and parachurch ministries to create new methods that work for all generations today. Some of the desired changes are warranted and would likely result in women maturing into spiritually healthy, all-in Christ-followers. Others could lead us down dangerous roads toward generations of biblically illiterate women, a devastating consequence of good intentions but flawed foresight. We wrote this book to help women leaders assess and implement needed changes in effective ministry to women, and to avoid grievous consequences that loom ahead if we miss the mark.

WE ALL NEED JESUS

Twenty-eight years old, attractive, and earning $95,000 a year writing software, Amy was estranged from her mother, never knew her father, and recently ended a four-year relationship with a live-in boyfriend. A coworker deposited her in my office with a plea: "Help her. She's missed two weeks of work and she can't stop crying."

As I (Sue) looked into Amy's swollen eyes, I saw myself thirty years earlier and remembered the hopelessness. But God had provided a spiritual mother named Kathy Hyde who nursed me back to health by introducing me to Jesus and re-parenting me as I learned to lean on him. Their love transformed me. When I reflect on the difference Jesus has made in my life over the past half-century, gratitude overwhelms me.

Now I am the spiritual mother. But will the same methods and models used to help me work for Amy? Yes and no. Amy and I were both in our twenties when we turned to Christ for help. We shared the same fundamental need—an intimate relationship with Jesus. We needed to know the Bible, to enjoy being part of his family. We needed women to model what a godly woman looked like. We needed a push to risk ministering to others in a way that complemented our design and gifts. Our needs may have been the same, but what worked for me thirty years ago will *not* work for Amy. Why? Amy is a postmodern woman.

What does that mean? Kelley and I wrote this book to answer that question, and to show you how to include Amy in your ministry.

HOW TO USE THIS BOOK

Part 1: The Transformation Model and Why It's Working

Part 1 characterizes the postmodern woman to help you understand her mindset. You must know who she is before you can reach her. The term "postmodern" characterizes the worldview of generations labeled Gen X (1965–1979), Millennial (1980–1994), and Gen Z (1995–early 2000s). But be cautious that you don't exclude any generation as you attempt to woo one specific group. We'll address these issues and show you how to minimize the pitfalls.

We also introduce you to the Transformation Model. This model meets the needs of today's women, both modern and postmodern. We will examine seven pillars of the model that work whether you minister in the church, on campuses, or around the world. In part 1, we examine this model in general terms. Later, in parts 2, 3, and 4, we'll adapt these pillars and principles to specific areas of ministry.

Part 2: Taking the Transformation Model to the Church

In part 2, we'll examine what's happening in the church and how to apply the Transformation Model there. More and more women are assuming leadership roles in the church. Initially churches and parachurch ministries hired women to lead children or women. But when supervisors observed the excellent gifts, abilities, and work ethics of many of these women, they opened doors for them to lead all kinds of other ministries. Today you are more likely to find women serving in a wide variety of positions.

Church leaders have come to understand the Titus 2 mandate that women are responsible for the spiritual growth of the women in their churches. Women attend staff meetings and enjoy their place on the team. More churches pay their women what men in comparable positions make. Some still do not.

Women in smaller churches observe the exciting ministries in the megachurches and struggle to attain the same effectiveness despite their lack of resources. Most small churches cannot afford to bring on staff a minister/ pastor to women (or any other assistant pastor position), so women labor as lay ministers with hopes that their pastors value their work, trusting that they are doing what they can with what they have.

Whether you already serve on staff or as a lay minister, these principles will help you build a ministry that works today. We will show you how to implement these ideas in your setting, both small and large churches. One size does not fit all, but the same principles apply everywhere.

Part 3: Taking the Transformation Model to the Campus

Part 3 takes the Transformation Model to the campus, where women of all ages desire training. Colleges, universities, and seminaries are packed with women preparing for ministry.[1] Wherever women congregate they want to connect. But the exclusive sorority model grates against Christ's ways. Women are instituting different organizations on campuses that will address the specific needs of women there. Discover these and explore how to begin a ministry to women on your campus.

Part 4: Converting the Transformation Model Cross-Culturally

Finally, in part 4, we will take the Transformation Model to the mission field. Is it applicable to other cultures? Absolutely! But missionaries must tweak these principles to fit the culture and contexts where they serve.

For centuries women missionaries blazed trails in other lands. They evangelized, planted churches, taught, and worked in medicine. Today they continue their noble labor. But now women also teach nationals how to minister to their women. Whether on short-term trips or long-term commitments, women equip their sisters around the world. We'll look at cross-cultural strategies that work today.

In Addition . . .

We'll share stories of women influencers in various ministry contexts. You will benefit from their varied experiences and accrued wisdom. We hope you will find inspiration from one or more of them as you pursue your own ministry. Whether you have years invested in women's lives or you hear a faint call and want to explore the possibilities, this book can help.

But before we examine the multifaceted world of women's ministry in the new millennium, let's take a look at where we've been.

WHERE WE'VE BEEN

Models of Women's Ministry in America

Women have ministered to one another through the centuries, but most of that ministry occurred informally. From the frontier days until the mid-1900s, women formed the heart of communities around the country. They visited over the fence while hanging out their laundry, birthed each other's babies, kept watch over the neighborhood or town children—no matter whose they were. Before our culture dismantled the nuclear family, women cooked, canned, and cried together. They trained the younger women by example.

Many women grew up in church. The Ten Commandments hung on the walls of every classroom and the Lord's Prayer began the school day. Please don't misunderstand. This was not the golden age for women. They often felt the brunt of prejudice and opportunities were limited. But sisterhood flourished and women were seldom alone.

In the mid- to late 1800s various models of women's ministry emerged that took on the flavor of the times. Here is what they looked like.

The Tea Party Model

Women gathered for social events and activities. They drank tea and enjoyed each other's company. At these gatherings, women were expected to behave with proper etiquette and propriety. Such opportunities provided excellent training for younger women, who learned social graces, and gave everyone a chance to show off that new hat.

Today, younger women still love to gather, but seldom for fashion shows or mother-daughter banquets. Instead you'll find them laughing and lounging on one another's sofas discussing streaming entertainment or working together in a food pantry. They love community but reject social events and activities that promote what they see as a false happy-church-face or "putting on airs." They value authenticity.

The Social Activism Model

Christian women of the nineteenth century valued service. The mid-1800s saw the rise of voluntary associations designed by and for women, dedicated to the betterment of American society. We will use two still-existing movements to illustrate this model.

As rural America gave way to the Industrial Revolution and the urban experience, women found themselves thrust into unfamiliar and sometimes dangerous territory on college campuses, in the factories, and on the streets. They needed support, training, and a place of refuge. In 1858, the Young Women's Christian Association (YWCA) began providing boardinghouses for young working women, political lobbying for better working conditions and equal protection under the law (remember: women could not vote until the 1920s), and a variety of recreational activities for these young women living away from home. The YWCA gave women an opportunity to serve other women on a broader social stage.

In 1874, women concerned about the destructive power of alcohol founded the Women's Christian Temperance Union (WCTU). They met in churches to pray, and then marched to the saloons to ask the owners to close their establishments. Women drove the push to make Prohibition law. But behind the WCTU's temperance reform was "protection of the home." Through education and example, the women of WCTU hoped to encourage total abstinence from alcohol, and later, tobacco and recreational drugs. Today, the WCTU remains active in the fight against drug and alcohol abuse.

These organizations, and others like them, arose out of a biblically-based concern for the welfare of women and families. The founding women had a knowledge of Christ and the Bible. Postmodern women rarely have that foundation of faith. However, younger women today tend to value social justice and community activism like their nineteenth-century ancestors. If you want younger women to join you, you'll need to include community and social activism opportunities because these women expect to live out what they learn in the Scriptures.

The Missions Model

Until the 1980s, women called by God served on the foreign mission field because they found few meaningful opportunities to serve God in American churches. As a result, churches designed programs to learn about women missionaries and support them. Today, however, the comprehensive reach of media enables women to embrace a global perspective even in their faith. Many desire to help women around the world, but they also need to heal before they can focus on others.

While women's ministries must foster a global perspective, missions should serve as an arm, not the core, of every women's ministry. We cannot help others until we are healed ourselves. But watch out—when today's woman experiences healing, she doesn't just want to learn about missions. She wants to *do* missions.

The Parachurch Bible Study Model

Women love to study the Bible. But because churches did not provide the opportunity, Bible studies outside the church began to flourish in the 1950s. Bible Study Fellowship and other Bible classes exploded, attracting women from all denominations and backgrounds. I (Sue) came to Christ in a parachurch Bible study. The teacher became my spiritual mother, and she taught me to teach the Bible. I served as a teaching leader and teacher trainer in Dallas-based Bible Discussion Groups, Inc. for more than fifteen years and considered this ministry my spiritual home. More than my church, it nourished, fed, and challenged me.

These parachurch studies provide valuable equipping opportunities for women in churches without women's ministries. But churches are meant to serve women more holistically. For within the church, as we teach and help women mature, we walk with them in a variety of other arenas. We give women varied opportunities to use their gifts in the service of the body of Christ. We partner with other ministries. We participate in God's key instrument on earth—the church.

The One-Size-Fits-All Model

Churches used to schedule women's activities and Bible studies during the day. The vast majority of women were married and stayed home, even after their children grew up and moved away. Not so today. Now over half of women are single (53.2 percent in 2016),[2] and almost 60 percent work full or part time.[3]

America has been described as a "melting pot" where different races, nationalities, and genders are expected to conform and think alike. Women in church today don't resemble a melting pot. They look more like a green salad. They look and think differently. They like to be distinct. Many enjoy variety and request to be with women of different ages and stages.

The 2010 census found 13.1 million households headed by single women. Three out of five children in the United States are in childcare.[4] What are the demographics in your church?

Women ministering in the new millennium serve every woman or they neglect their call. That complicates everything we do. As a result, we change our meeting times and formats to honor working women's schedules. Teachers learn to use illustrations that aren't always about the stay-at-home mom with 2.2 children. We intentionally remember singles. Our workshops address issues besides training toddlers and surviving teens. No longer does one size fit all in the church, but variety adds zest and spice to our work. The challenge can be a blessing if we choose to see it that way.

HOW DO YOU FEEL ABOUT WHAT YOU HAVE JUST READ?

As you contemplate the different models, do you observe any that dominate your ministry? Most women's ministries today can identify with aspects of each model.

But the overall flavor of your ministry should no longer reflect any of these outdated models. In our churches, we changed gradually, as the church was also transitioning. Change can be a painful process. Approach it with wisdom and a gentle spirit. The sign on our missions minister's door read, "Blessed are the flexible for they will not get bent out of shape." If you tend toward inflexibility, we suggest any of these:

William Bridges, *Managing Transitions, Make the Most of Change.* Reading, MA: Perseus Books, 1993.

Chip Heath and Dan Heath, *Switch: How to Change Things When Change Is Hard.* New York: Broadway Books, 2010.

John P. Kotter, *Leading Change.* Boston: Harvard Business School Press, 1996.

Keep in step with your supervisors, but remember that God may call *you* to point the way. Although change brings challenges, we have found God faithful when we knew he was leading us. Get on your knees, and if you are sure, enact change with God's blessing and strength. Remember: your changing may win women to Christ for eternity. And that's the bottom line.

A Woman of Influence
JENNIE ALLEN
by Amanda Sherzer

Jennie Allen's passion for making disciples began soon after she surrendered her life to Christ at age seventeen. She remembers, "I came home from Kanakuk Kamp filled with the Spirit and started teaching the Bible to younger high school girls."

She knew early on God was calling her to ministry, but she had no idea how this calling would play out. She simply had an innate "fire to give God away" to women. She taught her Bible in dorms and living rooms and invested in those God placed in front of her.

Reflecting on the audacious ways God has used her over the years, Jennie shares, "I fell into everything." He created unexpected avenues for her to make more disciples through writing books and Bible studies, teaching Scripture worldwide, and founding IF:Gathering, a movement inspired by her question: *If God is real . . . then what?*

IF is comprised of women who long for their lives to make an eternal difference. Jennie explained, "We don't want to just say, 'Yes, God is real.' We want to come together as a generation and live out what he has called us to do." At the center of IF stands discipleship, the way Jennie and her team believe God will change the world and reconcile it to himself. IF's staff, interns, and thousands of local leaders provide women with resources and events to help them learn more about God and how to disciple others in their spheres. These efforts have resonated mightily. Since IF's launch in 2013, it has reached more than one million people in 179 countries.

Jennie never expected IF to explode so quickly. She readily admits she and her team did not have intricate strategies or marketing plans when they began; they built IF through surrender and obedience to God. They worked hard and trusted as he guided them through the little and the big. "We prayed for God to lead, and we followed him the best we could, one step at a time."

Jennie credits the Holy Spirit for IF's effectiveness as he has reached and ministered to its wide audience through its gatherings and tools. She also knows IF would not have flourished without the army of people who work alongside her. "We're not meant to do this alone. I'm such a big believer in the body of Christ."

She advises women to likewise link arms with other Christ-followers. "If you start a Bible study—even if it's seven people—ask a friend to help." She also urges leaders to chase service rather than perfection, seeking to please God instead of living in fear of messing up before man. "Women don't have to prove themselves to others," she says.

Jennie observes how some people believe they need an official ministry job to make an impact for God. She counters, "We make it too complicated! The pursuit of souls is not a 'profession.' You don't need a title. We're *all* called to pour our lives into ministry. We're *all* called to make disciples."

Jennie Allen graduated from Dallas Theological Seminary in 2005 with a master's in biblical studies. She is the author of the best-selling books *Anything, Restless,* and *Nothing to Prove,* and the Bible studies *Stuck, Chase, Restless,* and *Proven.* The founder and visionary of IF:Gathering, Jennie lives in Dallas, Texas, with her husband, Zac, and their four children.

PART I

THE TRANSFORMATION MODEL AND WHY IT'S WORKING

Chapter 1

WHO IS THE POSTMODERN WOMAN?

The phenomenon of the generation gap reaches beyond familial relationships—mothers and daughters, grandfathers and grandsons—into the church body. Older women, content with their traditional, didactic method of Bible study, sometimes feel confused or threatened by the younger generation's desire for a more organic approach, creativity, diversity, and spontaneity. "We know our way works—why change it?" they wonder. Older women sometimes ask me (Sue), "What in the world do these younger women mean by *organic*?" Dallas Theological Seminary (DTS) adjunct professor Barbara Neumann explains the concept well in our book *Organic Mentoring*.

> The organic movement started as a means to produce natural food but eventually grew into a belief system, one that is embraced by many next generation people. Organic elements shape their values and lifestyles in many ways. This belief system leads young people to a simpler, more natural and authentic way of life. It moves away from outside control, artificial ingredients, and synthetic products.
>
> When we understand that the organic belief system also extends to the way Postmoderns relate to others, we begin to *get* them. Their relationships unfold naturally according to their own timetables. When we talked candidly with young women in our research, they all wished the mentoring process could be more "organic." When they look at the way we traditionally structure mentoring, they don't see organic. They see layers of additives that make the process feel unnatural. (*Organic Men-*

toring, A Mentor's Guide to Relationships with Next Generation Women, Sue Edwards and Barbara Neumann, Grand Rapids, MI: Kregel Publications, 2014, pp. 97, 98)

Younger and middle-aged women observe their mothers and grandmothers in church and say, "Boring! That is *not* for me." They walk away from relevant truth because they can't relate to an antiquated method. Many postmoderns believe they have little in common with the moderns—an unfortunate and potentially destructive misconception.

These labels don't fit each individual. Many women in their sixties think like postmodern women. And young women who grew up in Christian homes often take on the attributes of modern women. But for the sake of our discussion, these labels work. They help us as we search for methods to bring the generations together.

DO YOUR METHODS REACH THE POSTMODERN WOMAN?

Many postmoderns view life from a different perspective than moderns—yet many women attempting ministry use obsolete methods that won't work with young women. Highly structured formats, academic Bible teaching without application, and simplistic thinking don't interest the digital generations. These women seek authentic relationships and "spirituality," but not packaged in yesterday's styles.

The postmodern woman wants transformation. She wants genuine relationships and deep spiritual experiences. She demands we address the complexities of life and refuses to settle for pat answers and superficial explanations, insisting that we take off our masks and get real. She wants substantial change—a new life that works.

Many hurt deeply and fear trusting anyone. These are the daughters of radical feminism. They come to the church searching for authentic community and family.

Many call several women "mom" and several men "dad." Adults played musical chairs in their lives, so they learned independence for survival. They experienced the emptiness of isolation and are desperate to connect. And so they come to Jesus. We must seriously consider their needs as we plan our ministries. But we must understand the challenges as we seek to woo and win them.

BE ALERT TO THE CHALLENGES

Don't Marginalize or Unnecessarily Offend Moderns

Imagine the results if we changed our methods to attract young women but lost the older women in the process. Our challenge is to embrace the postmodern woman while retaining the generations of women who came before her. Why? Because these earlier generations are our army of spiritual mothers. They will teach and train the younger women God is sending us. They will enfold postmoderns when the leaders run out of arms. Only a fool would fashion a ministry to the needs of one generation and forget the other.

Don't Capitulate to the Culture

Aspects of both modern and postmodern cultures fly in the face of biblical truth. For example, typical postmoderns believe truth is relative. Secular education is founded on that premise, affecting every academic discipline. But the Bible teaches absolute truth. In our attempts to attract postmoderns, should we abandon teaching absolute truth because they resist? Absolutely not. That would be capitulating to postmodern culture.

But we can teach biblical truth using methods that appeal to postmoderns. How? By using more stories, images, and art—and by making the main points of our messages applicational rather than academic. Postmoderns aren't impressed that we can conjugate Greek verbs. First, they want to know if our faith works.

Modernism also contradicts Scripture. For example, in the past, relationships and families have been sacrificed on the altar of modernity's materialism. Dr. Alice Mathews, former Lois W. Bennett Associate Professor of Educational and Women's Ministries at Gordon-Conwell Theological Seminary, comments:

> Having done some useful course work and a lot of reading in my Ph.D. studies on postmodernism, I see many great dangers in modernism as well as in postmodernism. So I see myself as a "pre-modern" woman living in the midst of the ongoing assumptions of modernity and almost welcoming postmodernism as a way of forcing Christians to see how much we've bought into the culture of modernity in community-destroying ways. No, I am

not postmodern. But nothing less than postmodern thought could force us to question the tenets of modernity which are in the air we breathe. I know that I bought into modernity for the first six decades of my life, and only in the last decade I have come to see how that ethos, modernity, has been at odds with the gospel of our Lord Jesus Christ.[5]

Do you consider the needs of postmodern women in your ministry? If not, is it time for a change? But be careful not to capitulate to either culture or unnecessarily offend either group as you do.

Awaken to the Need for Change

To answer my calling I (Sue) have been forced to change. Why? Because it's not about me—it's about them!

I will never forget attending a women's ministry conference at Multnomah Bible College and Seminary in Portland, Oregon. Before me sat a panel of Christian women, all under thirty, most of whom studied in the women's ministry track. Several had grown up in Christian homes and the others came to Christ through youth ministry or in their early twenties. I listened intently as they answered questions that revealed a different worldview than mine. One raised in a Christian home expressed that she felt disenfranchised from her generation. But she also looked at the world differently from her mother. She felt caught between two worlds. Others identified with their generation and talked about their struggle to see life "biblically." Each one challenged us to understand them and their lost generation.

A modern woman once asked me, "Why should I change? Why can't the postmoderns change instead?" Former Dallas Theological Seminary (DTS) student Amy Joy Warner has an answer.

> For the Christian, Jesus Christ offers the ultimate example for approaching the postmodern culture. John, in his Gospel, clearly illuminates Jesus's method when he writes, "The Word became flesh and made his dwelling among us" (1:14). In Jesus Christ, God approached humanity in terms it could understand. In doing so, God established a pattern for those who would

follow after Christ. God's incarnation creates the necessity and appropriateness of a postmodern approach to Christian ministry. If we are to follow his example, we have no excuse for not accommodating ourselves to the postmodern culture in such a way that Christ is evident once again.

The postmodern women at the conference came to faith because someone reached out to them in terms they could understand. I left the conference knowing God was calling me to change the way I approached women's ministry.

IS JESUS ASKING YOU TO CHANGE?

We need a different model because traditional models, as we have shown, don't reach the postmodern world in which we now live. God loves this world and asks us to woo them to him. Jesus's last words on earth are still our chief concern.

> Therefore go and make disciples of all nations, baptizing them in the name of the Father and of the Son and of the Holy Spirit, and teaching them to obey everything I have commanded you. (Matt. 28:19–20)

God calls us to reach all nations, all peoples, all generations. As God brings these postmodern women into our churches, Titus 2:3–5 serves as the foundational text for ministry to women.

Background

After Paul planted churches, normally he left disciples behind to shepherd the new flocks. In Crete, Paul left Titus and continued to mentor him through correspondence. One of his letters included instructions to various groups. He wrote specifically concerning women:

> Likewise, teach the older women to be reverent in the way they live, not to be slanderers or addicted to much wine, but to teach what is good. Then they can urge the younger women to love

their husbands and children, to be self-controlled and pure, to be busy at home, to be kind, and to be subject to their husbands, so that no one will malign the word of God. (Titus 2:3–5)

Identify "Mature" Women

First, Titus needed to identify "older" women and delegate the care of other women in the church to them. The Greek word for "older" denotes the idea of being "advanced in the process." In contrast, "younger" women carries with it the idea of being recent, or early, new in the process. These terms don't necessarily mean chronological age but can also relate to spiritual age. This is important because younger women mature in Christ qualify for leadership. Paul was advising Titus to delegate and prepare spiritually mature women to shepherd other women.

Cretan women rarely enjoyed educational opportunities, but Paul instructed Titus to disregard this cultural norm, to find women who distinguished themselves by their love for the Lord, and to prepare them to minister to other women.

Paul's letter to Titus expressed real urgency. In 2:1, he insisted, "You, however, must teach what is appropriate to sound doctrine." The health and survival of the church depended on equipping its people, including women, and on growing both strong men and strong women, enabling them to persevere in the midst of a hostile Cretan environment. Paul's words were not a suggestion but a command. Churches today include many fine ministries that are not specifically commanded in Scripture. Ministry to women, however, is mentioned clearly.

Titus's Temporary Role

Titus's role included priming the pump for women, getting the ministry off the ground. After Titus identified and equipped these "older" women, they would be ready to teach, train, and mentor the generation behind them. Imagine if Paul's mandate had been common practice in all churches since the first century!

Paul provided guidelines to help Titus know how to identify women advanced in the process. Who is a Titus 2 woman? What core qualities did Paul elevate that we still need to value today? Of course, no woman reflects these values perfectly, but she should be seeking these attributes and should have achieved a measure of maturity before she's trusted to lead others. Also, women who seriously desire to prepare themselves for effective ministry must intentionally develop these qualities.

Three Qualifications for Ministering to Women

First, Paul advised Titus to find women who were "reverent in the way they live." We must live out our love for the Lord as a lifestyle, a real walk with God, no masks—what you see in public reflects who you are in private.

Next, Paul focused on two key negatives. The first: "not to be slanderers." Do you struggle to overcome a loose tongue? Proverbs 13:3 instructs, "Those who guard their lips preserve their lives, but those who speak rashly will come to ruin."

Don't be like the woman who backed into another car. She wrote a note and put it under the windshield wiper of the damaged car that read, "*I have just smashed your car. The people who saw the accident are watching me. They think I am writing down my name and address. They are wrong.*"

Only women who habitually use truthful, honest, wise words qualify for ministry. Our words play a mammoth part in our effectiveness in ministry and our legacy. Slanderers let a loose tongue do its damage, talking too much, gossiping, failing to keep a confidence. In ministry, you will be privy to secrets that can ruin other people's lives. The Greek word for slander carries the meaning of joining the work of the devil to undermine and destroy. If we slander others, we sow discord and discredit ourselves. It's an integrity issue, one of your most prized possessions. So take this admonition seriously and get a good grip on your tongue.

Paul also insisted that a Titus 2 woman not be "addicted to much wine." Obviously, this prohibits the overuse of alcohol, but it also represents a much broader problem then and now—addictions and distractions of all kinds. What helps women escape pain? Examples include food, technology, shopping, unhealthy romantic and sexual relationships, perfectionism, exercise, and prescription drugs. In extremes, these issues are idols, and we'll battle these idols until Jesus returns. But when women learn God's Word together, love one another well, pray for each other, and hold one another accountable, these addictions and distractions lose their power.

The Two Key Elements of a Transformational Ministry to Women

Next, the text reveals two core elements. What are we supposed to do to help one another grow up in Jesus? A Titus 2 ministry to women must run on two separate tracks.

First, it must include gifted women teachers called to teach "what is good" (Titus 2:3). Paul uses the Greek term for a formal teacher, one who infuses other women with sound, healthy instruction. This word described rabbis and doctors, people who healed or taught truth and practical wisdom. God calls some of us to formally teach, proclaim, and herald the Word of God. We teach with humility in the sense of this C. S. Lewis quote: "Think of me as fellow patient in the same hospital who having been admitted a little earlier could give some advice."[6]

Paul alerts us to a second priority when he says in verse 4, "Then they can train . . ." The Greek word for train does not denote formal teaching, but rather the cultivation of common sense or wisdom, skill in living. We need an army of women, advanced in the process, to come alongside others as mentors, coaches, and spiritual advisors to model an authentic Christian life.

Training can be one-on-one or in a group. It's life-on-life, everyday practical skills to help us navigate this difficult world. A hundred years ago, many women grew up in Christian homes surrounded by large extended families. They mentored one another naturally, but few experience this today. We need more intentional mentoring cultures where these kinds of interactions naturally occur.

But to make this reality, we need intergenerational interaction in our ministries. We need touch points to bring together women of different ages. Titus 2 assumes this dynamic, and in ancient churches it naturally happened, but today many of our churches seldom facilitate intergenerational interaction in meaningful ways. To intentionally create ministries that reflect the truths in Titus 2, consider reading Sue and Barbara Neumann's book, *Organic Mentoring: A Mentor's Guide to Relationships with Next Generation Women* (Kregel, 2014).

Topics to Teach

In verses 4 and 5, Paul provides a list of topics to teach, important then and now. However, in Crete most women were married, often as young teens in arranged marriages. Today women need a wider curriculum. Many women remain single longer or permanently, and a large percentage work outside the home. These women also need biblical literacy and life skills for today's world. We minister to a much more diverse group of women than Titus did.

Expected Result

Verse 5 says we live out Titus 2:3–5, "so that no one will malign the word of God." Malign means to speak evil of or give false reports. Do people malign the Bible today? Absolutely. We don't know exactly how this works, but when people see biblically literate Christian women living out what they know, serving with integrity in their families, workplaces, and communities, and raising up one another, somehow, God is glorified and Jesus looks good.

HOW DO MODERNS VIEW THE WORLD?

Both modernism and postmodernism strive to make meaning of the cultural, economic, political, and social changes taking place in art, architecture, literature, the social sciences, popular culture, industry, business, technology, and education. Modernism is committed to logic, reason, and the scientific method and assumes that these are the tools that lead to truth and reality. Modernists have long believed that the scientific method is capable of producing solutions to the problems of the world and that there are no limits to where the search for truth may lead.

They equate change with progress and believe that democracy leads to freedom, equality, justice, and prosperity. For modernists, education and professionalism are seen as keys to upward mobility and the attainment of the American Dream. But there is a darker side to modernism, which is the object of much of the criticism aimed its way by the postmodernists. Modernism has produced rampant materialism, a consumer society, a ravaged environment, and unrestrained technology. It can be associated with oppression, exploitation, repression, violence, and even terror.[7]

For many postmoderns, previous generations have not solved the world's problems. Science and technology have not provided the answers. They are right. But neither will secular postmodern philosophy give them the answers they seek. What is true for moderns is also true for postmoderns, and all people who ever lived or will live—only Jesus can fill the need in their souls.

Nevertheless, postmodern thinking has turned our world upside down. Len Sweet writes, "A flood tide of a revolution is cutting its swath across our world and is gathering prodigious momentum."[8] We must view our world as a postmodern world.

So, ready or not . . . if we desire to have a successful ministry to today's woman, we must change our tactics to win her. We must approach her in a way she can understand. What characterizes the postmodern woman?

FOUR ATTRIBUTES OF THE POSTMODERN WOMAN

I observe postmodernism in the women I teach at the seminary and minister to in our church. I see these trends in the media and in my neighbors. I now consider these factors as I prepare to teach the Bible and design courses.

1. "Double Loop Thinking"

Many postmodern woman have learned to feel comfortable believing two contradictory ideas at the same time and not be bothered by the contradiction. They believe our ability to understand truth is limited, so when faced with different facets of opposing truth, they ignore the inconsistencies. Life is so fast and full of mystery that many postmoderns believe they cannot comprehend it. For example:

- They live in an "in your face" but "get out of my face" society.[9]
- The company that markets the sexiest lingerie also promotes "Victorian" ambiance.[10]
- Technology pulls us together while pulling us apart.
- They think community and global at the same time.
- They are connected through technology but fascinated with the past.
- They love extremes but find simplicity attractive.
- They are closed off from the world by the internet, yet time online only makes them want to go to Australia—and they go.

2. Three Times HOT

High-Online Technology

High-Online Technology (HOT) has three distinct meanings for the postmodern. More has changed in the past fifty years than in the past five hundred years. Remember that our changing times parallel the transition from the medieval era to the modern era.[11] It is estimated that more information has been generated in the past three decades than in the previous five thousand years. One weekday edition of *The New York Times* contains more information than the average person encountered in an entire lifetime in seventeenth-century England.[12] The internet has changed our world.

I (Sue) have a love-hate relationship with technology. I love the services it performs as I write to you, but I hate when my computer acts up. It took me years to love texting, and I'm still slow. But Kelley, for instance, is at home behind the screen. To connect with younger women I must be HOT(ter).

Regarding the rapid advancements in technology, consider the following, written in our 2002 edition:

> Do you realize that if your car is less than ten years old, it has at least thirty computers in it? Already some textbooks are on-line and updated daily. If you have a digital watch, it contains more computing power than existed in the world before 1962. Speech recognition systems can identify 230,000 words with 95 percent accuracy. Think of the changes in technology when voice activation becomes standard. Before long your computer will speak, your TV will listen, and your telephone will show you pictures. There's a cartoon in which a man says to his wife, "Answer the TV, honey, I'm watching the phone."[13]

Every one of these predictions is reality today. The way technology is changing our world leaves us breathless. We need to stay connected, or we will be out of touch. Consider the explosion of online spiritual resources such as podcasts, Bible studies, social media, blogs, and videos that many people use to supplement their spiritual walk.

Hands-on Truth

Postmoderns grew up learning that there was no absolute truth. Secular education assumes this fact and most postmoderns don't question it. They will go to the wall for a few principles—animal rights, the environment, and freedom of speech—but generally the concept of truth is hard for them.[14] As a result they aren't easily reached by intellectual, linear arguments. The evangelist will need more than principles and propositions to win the postmodern. This is bad news for those of us who love truth and were trained to communicate it through propositions, three points, and a poem. Those skills will help us, but we need more.

Does this mean we no longer teach truth? Not at all. The postmodern needs truth desperately. We must continue teaching the Bible but not just sprinkling in topical tidbits of truth out of context. Trends in women's materials seem to take us in that direction. These approaches have quick appeal, but like junk food, they're not nourishing if we want to see real spiritual growth in women. We will address the necessity to teach the Bible book by book and in context later.

We must adapt our teaching methods to reach the postmodern mind, remembering that moderns also sit listening. We will dig into these methods in part 2.

"Hands-on Truth" requires that we live out the principles we teach *before* we expect our listeners to believe us. Above all other criteria, a postmodern ministry must be relational. First and foremost, Christians must show themselves to be fully integrated personally. Mayers asserts that John 17 is the most distinctive of many texts that call for Christians to be authentic in word and deed, i.e., lifestyle. Jesus is praying that the oneness he shares with the Father might be the same kind of oneness that we share within our own persons. There is to be no artificialness or hypocrisy! Christians must be truly caring, genuine, transparent. It is for such irrefutable authentic lives, not cold rationalistic assertions, that Jesus prays. Jesus wants us set apart in truth. That is our outward claim is identical with our inward reality.[15]

When the postmodern observes consistency in our lives, then we begin to earn the opportunity to engage in dialogue with her about the hope that we have.

Sweet writes that postmoderns are "dealers in love more than dealers in dogma. But in classic double-ring fashion, postmodern culture needs more truth, not less. The difference is that Truth is not a principle or a proposition but a Person. Truth is not rules and regulations but a relationship. God did not send a statement but a Savior."[16]Although biblical truths are stated and learned as propositions and principles, at the heart of Christianity stands a relationship with Jesus.

High on Touch

Postmoderns want experience, relationships, community, and interaction. Not content to sit and listen to someone speak to them, they want to participate. Many postmoderns are desperate for relationships.

During the panel discussion at the Oregon conference, the young women continually used the word *home*. Those who grew up without faith kept reiterating, "We never really had a home." "We want to know what a home feels like." "Could you make us part of your home?" Not only do they enjoy being invited into someone's home, but they also seek healthy, intimate relationships. They want to be touched—physically, emotionally, and spiritually. They want to belong.

Postmoderns think that hunger will be satisfied by belonging to a community of people. They don't understand that only a relationship with Christ quenches our spiritual thirst. While they are learning, we envelop them in our authentic community to show them the difference Christ makes in our relationships. And there we teach them the truth—not only about Jesus, but also all the other truths from God's Word. To embrace them we need an army of arms that are HOT—High on Touch. We need women from multiple generations to surround the mass of postmodern women seeking Christ, to reach out and embrace them where they live.

To reach the postmodern woman, we need to be HOT—High-Online Technology, Hands-on Truth, and High on Touch.

3. Chaord

Author Len Sweet coined this unusual term, meaning a mixture of chaos and order. As a modern woman I learned that chaos was bad, and order was next to godliness. I love structure. When my daughter Rachel studied on her bed with the radio playing in the background, I would insist she turn off the music and sit at her desk. The next day I would find her on her bed again, background music playing away. The battle raged until I heard an expert teach on different learning styles. I recognized that my daughter's learning style differed from mine. I learned to let her study in ways that worked for her.

I have also observed that her generation is more comfortable in chaos. The world is so complex that they are used to several things going on at once. They seem to like it. They exist within the tension of order and chaos with far greater ease than my generation. Flexibility comes more naturally to the postmodern woman.

I have learned to look at ministry not as a rigid organization but rather as an organism that moves and bends in response to its environment. We are no longer wedded to methods out of habit or tradition. Now we try to adapt when appropriate. Of course, we never change the foundations of our ministry—our commitment to teach God's Word and to live out Titus 2—but now we value creative ways to better serve all the generations.

We call it *chaord*—a willingness to function without such rigid walls of structure. We will address the practical details of this concept in part 2.

4. Spiritual Hunger

"For the first time in US history, we are in the midst of a massive spiritual awakening that the Christian church is not leading. Americans are exhibiting the highest interest in spiritual matters in fifty years and Christianity is registering the least amount of interest and energy in fifty years."[17] For believers that is frightening. I grew up learning that science would solve all our problems and give us all the answers. People who believed in a real God or a real devil were considered ignorant in my childhood home. Over sixty years later, we now enjoy the comforts science and medicine bring, but we know the limits of science. Where do Americans go for answers?

Postmoderns look to engage with the spiritual. Many embrace various forms of spirituality without identifying with a faith in God. In a recent Barna Research study, 93 percent of those who defined themselves as "spiritual" hadn't attended a religious service in the past six months. Postmoderns want to know God, but they look suspiciously at organized "religion." They don't trust bureaucracy, government, organizations, and institutions—or anything remotely traditional. Barna Research believes "this group of *the spiritual but not religious* display an uncommon inclination to think beyond the material and to experience the transcendent."[18]

While most integrate some form of spirituality in their lifestyle, not all are experiencing the benefits. In a recent study, Pew Research found only "sixty-four percent of religiously affiliated adults say they feel a deep sense of spiritual peace and well-being at least weekly, compared with only forty percent of those who are unaffiliated."[19] Not all who identify themselves as spiritual experience internal peace. This reveals the gap in longing for the spiritual and lacking relationship with Jesus Christ. Our goal is to hone in on their longing for the spiritual while enlightening them to the truth of the Scriptures. This compels our ministry to think about the ways we can draw in postmoderns.

Some fear that catering to a postmodern crowd will compromise the integrity of our ministry, making it unrecognizable. Not so! It's possible to adjust our methods to further our reach. In the first century, the early church sought to win souls and grow converts. The church met in homes, loosely connected (see Acts). Likewise, in a postmodern world, what outdated programs might we alter to woo young people? How can we adapt our ministry to appeal to their longing for God in the spiritual? We have spiritual food. Let's present this food in a way that is palatable, because we know it will nourish them now and forever. If we don't, they'll go elsewhere for the spirituality they crave. To minister to postmoderns, we need a new model.

A Woman of Influence
ROXY HOCKENSMITH
by Amanda Sherzer

Roxy Hockensmith works as the Director of Women's Ministry at McLean Bible Church (MBC) located right outside Washington, D.C. She understands the importance of her job because she understands the importance of women. "Women wear so many hats. They're great connectors. If you reach women and help them to know Christ, you'll reach so many people. You'll impact friends, husbands, and children."

That truth hits close to home for Roxy. When she was a girl, her mother converted from Islam to Christianity and started attending MBC. Even though Roxy had no interest in church, her mom signed her up for MBC's junior high camp. Roxy asked her camp counselor questions about Jesus for hours and decided to give her life to him that weekend. She went on to "practically live at McLean" during her teens. She recalled, "The women of the church helped raise me."

Roxy now devotes her life to pouring into other women. She shepherds them and equips them with the tools to know and obey God's Word. From organizing various mother's groups, mission trips, and events, to supervising Bible studies, Roxy is "one person overseeing a lot" as the only MBC women's ministry staffer. She explained, "Recruiting, training, and empowering volunteers is a huge part of my job. I look and pray for people who are as excited about women's ministry as I am."

In a church that draws 8,000–10,000 attendees each week, Roxy longs for every woman to feel known. She shared, "We want to make a large church feel small." She encourages women to find community by serving or joining a Bible study. Many of MBC's members travel frequently and work long days—or they have spouses who do. Providing childcare at gatherings and ways for people to connect online (such as by watching MBC's large group Bible study livestreamed on Facebook) helps keep women involved.

With around seventy-three countries represented at MBC, Roxy aims to invite diverse Christian speakers to events and offer special Bible studies. For example, Roxy—who is Iranian and speaks Farsi—recently began a study for Persian women.

She also regularly meets women for coffee and spends time in her office counseling. "Many woman don't feel comfortable confiding in a man. I'm grateful our pastors value women and my role in ministering to them."

After serving in her job for over two and a half years, Roxy offers a few pieces of advice for others who lead church women's ministries:

- Don't be afraid to advocate for your church's women in an assertive and grace-filled way to ensure they are included, represented, and served.
- Keep a running list of the women with whom you meet and counsel. This list shows proof of the important work you do.
- Set boundaries. "You don't have to go to everything! My relationship with God and my husband are most important, and I can't do it all."
- Find a group of four or five mature women at your church who can provide you with Godly counsel and support.
- Stay humble. "When I try to work in my own strength, I mess things up and burn out. If I work through God's strength, the ministry flourishes."

She declared, "I'm quirky. I don't have it all together. I don't take myself too seriously—but I take this calling and my job very seriously."

Chapter 2

WHAT IS THE TRANSFORMATION MODEL?

We need a ministry model that meets the needs of today's women, both modern and postmodern. We call this model the Transformation Model because it has one goal—life change in women for their joy and God's glory!

Postmodern women demand that our ministries offer authentic, substantial opportunities to grow and serve. But they wince at the highly structured, programmatic approaches of the past. They want a more natural, organic feel. They dislike the tendency of many ministries to women to focus just on themselves rather than also serving in their communities.

Moderns and postmoderns often have different definitions of "social justice." Moderns fear that including social justice in our ministries will ultimately draw us away from a gospel focus, similar to what occurred with so many mainline denominations at the turn of the twentieth century. Postmoderns see social justice as a biblical mandate, and ministry without concern and compassion for the poor and needy is self-centered.

Is it possible to hear the concerns and meet the needs of both modern and postmodern women? We believe it is, but it will take communication, understanding, and sacrificing preferences on both sides. What might this model offer women of all generations that they have not experienced before?

THE SEVEN PILLARS OF THE TRANSFORMATION MODEL

1. The Transformation Model Centers on Scripture

If we envision women's ministry as a wheel, the hub of the wheel is a woman's intimate relationship with Christ nurtured through a study of God's Word. Bible study is the primary activity of the ministry, the one component designed with all the women of the church in mind, if the Bible study centers on whole books or general themes in the Bible and not topical studies aimed at specific groups. The glorious Scriptures are written ultimately to meet the needs of all generations, allowing them to come together in obedience to the Titus 2 mandate.

All other ministries are the spokes of the wheel. These spokes give women opportunities to use what they have learned in God's Word. Within them, we narrow the focus and minister to women with specific needs.

The truths of Scripture nourish all women, for all their lives. We have found that when postmoderns finally discover absolute truth on which to build their lives, they love truth as much as moderns do. So, when a woman asks us how to get involved in women's ministries, we almost always direct her to Bible study. There she will find the spiritual food she needs. The only exceptions are women who are so spiritually or emotionally unhealthy that they need one-on-one care. Once they are ready we redirect them to the Bible study.

In the Gospel of Matthew, a Pharisee asks Jesus to place a priority on the commandments. In response, Jesus models this wheel, answering the lawyer with, "'Love the Lord your God with all your heart and with all your soul and with all your mind.' This is the first and greatest commandment. And the second is like it: 'Love your neighbor as yourself'" (22:37–39). Jesus reveals that God desires to transform us through our relationship with him so that he can transform our relationship with others, that they may be transformed also. The greatest transformation tool is the Bible!

2. The Transformation Model Builds Relationships

Although the Scriptures are the focus of a life-changing women's ministry, mere knowledge of the Bible is not the desired goal. Rather it is first a deeper relationship with God and then healthy, intimate relationships with other women.

Women love to connect—some more than others. On leadership style and personality tests, both of us come out task-oriented. At the Bible classes, I (Sue) enjoy people but I am there for Bible study! During my early years as a minister to women, I created a Bible study format heavy on task and light on fellowship—and I paid the price. Some of our more relational women left looking for genuine friendships. I have learned that God values relationship too.

He created the church so that we could belong to one another. When our ministries give women time to connect as well as meaningful tools to deepen their friendships, everyone is blessed. Most postmodern women demand it—even if they are more task-oriented. Many, because of their backgrounds, need spiritual mothering as well as exposure to genuine relationships. It gives them a sense of home and proves that Christianity works.

Women in higher education also yearn for connection. They need a relationship with Jesus first. But often they do not realize they have such a need. They will join in just to make meaningful friendships. Many university and seminary campuses lack a ministry that offers both a relationship with Christ and also with other women. We will talk about how to implement such a ministry in part 3.

Around the world, women have the same needs. Missionaries find that bonding between American teams and nationals is a number-one priority. Different languages and cultures complicate the relationships, but the basics don't change. Growing to love one another and building relationships is second only to centering on Scripture.

3. The Transformation Model Accommodates Differences

Segregating women by ages and categories violates the Titus 2 mandate in Scripture. Most women enjoy being with women from different backgrounds and life stages.

Consider these real-life examples:

- In a small group, a single woman sees the tears and hears the woes of a woman who married carelessly. The single woman thinks seriously about whether or not to accept an invitation from a nonbeliever at work who has invited her to dinner.

- A young mother shares her struggles with her strong-willed two-year-old. An older mother explains what worked in her child's life. She cautions her not to overreact and comforts her with the knowledge that all two-year-olds throw tantrums.
- An African American woman prays for a white woman's ailing mother. The white woman has never experienced the delight of sisterhood with a woman of a different race. Both are blessed. Both learn to empathize more readily with the other's perspective on current events.
- A working woman vents frustration at her boss's inappropriate advances—but she loves her job. A professional woman with thirty years' experience takes her aside and helps her discover her options. She provides resources that will help if necessary. And she prays with her.
- The mother of a prodigal connects with a young woman who resembles her daughter. Together they talk through some of the issues that have estranged them and the mother begins to understand her daughter in ways she never had before. The mother takes steps toward her daughter and in time the relationship is healed.

Despite these benefits of bringing different women together, some women resist the idea. One year, we lost a few young mothers from our group because they wanted to study with other young moms. The next year we offered a small group just for them. But we recruited two older mothers to lead it. As we prayed for ways to retain our young mothers, God brought us a woman with a heart to begin a supplemental "moms" ministry that provided additional connection for mothers of young children but did not remove them from the mixed study groups.

4. The Transformation Model Makes Every Minute Meaningful

We live in a 24/7, all-the-time world. Whether same-day delivery, online grocery orders and drop-off, or smartphones in our pockets and purses, our culture stays over-connected and overworked, but spiritually and emotionally under-nourished.

We wake up in a different world than the one in which we went to sleep. Change happens so fast, we can't learn about something before it is obsolete. The pace of life isn't healthy. When people come into the church, we want to offer them a haven where the rhythm slows down, where we make time to turn our thoughts to God, relationships, and meaningful endeavors. We want to rest and focus on what's really important in life. And we should.

But time is tricky in ministry today. Women won't tolerate wasting their time. They are busy, some women with almost no free time, and joining your ministry comes with great sacrifice. They schedule in only what they believe is valuable. You will only waste their time once—maybe twice. As a result, we must plan carefully to meet the high standard.

We do not advocate meaningless entertainment or attempts to outdo the competition. But women will only participate in a ministry that is covered in prayer, planned well, and expertly executed. It had better be worth their time.

But there is a twist! The postmodern woman doesn't want to be rushed. Too much structure makes her uncomfortable. For several years I used a bell in our Bible study to signal when it was almost time to finish our table discussion. I also used it in our prayer time to let the women know when we were going to move on to a new subject. Many of the younger women did not like that bell. Women today want to know the time is well planned, but they also want the flexibility to "let the Spirit lead" at times. We'll talk about ways to incorporate *chaord* in your format later while still making every minute meaningful.

5. The Transformation Model Builds Teams

Team expert Don Simmons defines a team as "an enthusiastic group of people with complementary skills and gifts who work together toward common purposes and have a high level of trust and accountability."[20] You need a team. Our world desperately needs Jesus. Are you praying that God will enlarge your influence and bring you women of all generations? When he does, you will need an army of women at your side. You will never be able to meet those needs by yourself.

Building a team and delegating the ministry means giving up control. And you will invest countless hours recruiting, training, and encouraging your team. They will need you to oversee—not micromanage—their work. As a result, many leaders refuse to put in the time up front to build teams.

Our experience has shown us that ministry to women requires teamwork. Even in a small church, one woman cannot know enough, serve enough, or manage enough to make it all happen. Besides, ministry in community witnesses to postmoderns. They won't be impressed at your one-woman show. No matter how gifted or passionate you are, ultimately you can't do it alone.

Lone Ranger Alert!

Wherever you work, you will always find lone rangers—women who insist on doing their own thing. They refuse to work with others. Instead of agonizing over their loss, learn to let them go. God probably can't use them to their full potential, but that is their choice.

6. The Transformation Model Adds Variety

Have you noticed the many options on grocery store shelves? One missionary who returned home on furlough was so overwhelmed by the vast array of choices, she wanted to flee the store. Do you wish life were simpler? Although many of us do, it isn't. Americans expect variety.

What does that mean for ministry? In the church and on the campus, women—especially postmoderns—expect a medley of ministries. However, your ministry will look different depending on your size. Small churches and campuses are foolish to overextend resources. But variety comes packaged in different ways. We'll examine when and how to add variety in later sections.

7. The Transformation Model Prepares for Conflict

"I can't believe the lies he is telling about our pastor," moaned Ellen, a seminary student who served on the missions committee of her church. She grieved over a conflict between the senior pastor and the missions pastor, Sam. What happened? The two leaders were mismatched from the beginning. Sam, a retired missionary, insisted on ministering "the way it had always been done." The senior pastor believed Sam's methods were outdated and ineffective.

For three years, they tried to work out their differences. The senior pastor sent Sam to training seminars. He suggested Sam plan a short-term missions trip to expose church members to missions. Sam refused. Nothing worked, and eventually Sam lost his position.

Even before his last day at the church, Sam began to slander the senior pastor. He invited each member of the missions committee to dinner and used the time to defend his position and attack the integrity and character of the senior pastor. Sam used words like "evil" and "dangerous."

Ellen and her husband had accepted Sam's invitation to dinner—and Ellen was devastated. She had invested years in missions only to see it near destruction due to the controversy. "What does God want me to do?" she asked.

Unfortunately, this scenario is common. Whether you minister in a church, on a campus, or on the mission field, you will encounter conflict. Even if you make wise decisions, not everyone will agree with you. Those who aren't prepared reap consequences that break hearts, drive women from ministry, and damage God's good name.

Conflict is like a country road: we never know where it will lead. Unless we prepare ahead, conflict will take us where we don't want to go.

Many women assume that they can avoid conflict by making everyone happy. They think that because we are Christians, we won't disagree. But no matter what we do, we can't make everyone happy. And believers do disagree, sometimes so fiercely they dishonor God and damage the church or ministry they love.

At Irving Bible Church (IBC), women who served with Sue signed a pledge that they would handle conflict biblically. They studied principles from Matthew 18 and equipped themselves beforehand so they would know how to respond when conflict erupts.

Part 2, *Taking the Transformation Model to the Church,* contains instruction and resources to help you learn the skill of conflict resolution. Although we direct this section at those in church ministry, women on the campus, on the mission field, or in other kinds of ministry will find it equally valuable. Learn to survive conflict without casualties.

These seven pillars of the Transformation Model—center on Scripture, build relationships, accommodate differences, make every minute meaningful, build teams, add variety, and prepare for conflict—are basic to ministering to both postmodern and modern women. Details follow to help you apply these principles. Are you called to the church, the campus, the mission field, or another facet of women's ministry? Maybe you have the opportunity to minister in several of these arenas. It is our heartfelt prayer that God will use the principles, stories, and pioneer profiles ahead to transform lives and bring unspeakable joy.

PART 2

TAKING THE TRANSFORMATION MODEL TO THE CHURCH

Over the past thirty years, the Transformation Model has emerged in cutting-edge ministries to women in American churches. You could fly around the country and visit a variety of exceptional ministries. Unfortunately, few of us have the time or resources for such a trip. But this book can help you design your own innovative ministry for both postmodern and modern women in your church.

Part 2 contains strategies and examples from experienced church leaders as well as our own ideas. Do you serve women in your church as a paid staff member? Or are you a lay leader with a passion to implement a dynamic women's ministry in your church even though you won't be financially compensated? Maybe you don't know if God is calling you, but you sense a gentle stirring in your soul when you envision yourself impacting women for Christ. No matter your circumstances, this section will show you how to get off to a great start.

Chapter 3

BEGIN RIGHT!

Women today find themselves facing different scenarios. How you begin and how you minister is shaped by the size of your church, the leadership's attitude toward women, and whether the church already has a women's ministry. In this chapter, we will explore several real-life examples, learn from their experiences, and then glean some principles that apply to everyone.

A LARGE CHURCH WITHOUT A "TRANSFORMING" WOMEN'S MINISTRY

I (Sue) planted my first women's ministry in this scenario, at a megachurch of ten thousand members in a large denomination. Because the church had no woman on staff due to the pastor's views on that matter, different lay women tried each year to organize the women of the church. Several circles met in homes. Volunteers hosted spectacular dinners and fashion shows. But the deep needs of women were not addressed. And each year after she concluded her term, a different lay leader left in disappointment. My immediate predecessor was so discouraged that we couldn't get her to join us when we implemented the Transformation Model. Her experience had been painful and she wanted nothing to do with women's ministry. Sadly, I have observed this pattern repeatedly. When women receive little training or support, they often leave, vowing "Never again!"

A New Beginning

Liz was an elder's wife. From experience in a former church, she knew the impact a thriving women's ministry could have on women—and she wanted it for her church. Despite being gifted leader, Liz hadn't used her gifts in the church because there were few opportunities for women with gifts of leadership and vision. Instead she started her own business and worked in community organizations.

But God sparked a passion in her heart to begin a ministry that would transform women in her church. After brainstorming with local women experienced in ministry, she formed her plan, made an appointment with the pastor, and received his blessing. He even gave her a budget and a staff member as the women's ministry liaison. God was laying the foundation, and Liz's enthusiasm grew.

A New Team

The Sunday my family joined Liz's church, Liz ran down the aisle and embraced me. Immediately her women's ministry plans spilled out. She heard I just graduated from seminary. She knew I was an experienced Bible teacher. Would I join her? My passion reflected her passion and we felt God's timing. Liz and I teamed up for the next seven years.

We recruited women to pray. Liz knew those who had a heart for women. She met with each one and shared her vision. Then she asked them to consider joining us for periodic prayer.

Ten of us prayed together every other week over the next six months. We asked God for guidance on the structure of the ministry. We asked for leaders. We asked for God to send us the women to participate. We asked for credibility so that the leadership would ultimately hire a woman director. We understood that without a trained leader to bring consistency to the ministry, it would not flourish long-term—and our church had the resources to bring a woman on staff. We committed the entire ministry to him. In addition to prayer, we dreamed about a women's ministry uniquely designed for our church and what it would take for that dream to come true.

During those six months, God revealed the hearts and gifts of the women who faithfully prayed with us, and they became the new women's ministry board. The foundation for a team was laid.

This step is crucial. However long you prepare, a time of prayer and planning will provide a solid foundation for your future ministry. Don't skip this important element!

Who Are Your Women?

In most large churches, you will minister to women of all ages, stages, and backgrounds. You must consider these differences even as you plan for the first year. It is important not to grow too quickly, however. Focus on the core of your ministry first.

How can you learn the demographics of women in your church? If you have been a part of the church for many years, you may be familiar enough with its makeup. If not, ask a staff member. Those charged with integrating new members or with publicity may know statistics that would help you.

Consider using surveys. When a woman fills out a survey she knows you care about what she thinks. Free online tools such as Survey Monkey allow you to email individual attendees with short questionnaires. Let technology help you. However you do it, find out who your women are. Otherwise, you can't plan an effective ministry for them.

Invite Leaders' Wives

As we began, it was important to enlist as many staff and deacon wives as possible. We hosted a lovely lunch for them and introduced them to the ministry. Some joined in. Many did not. One hindrance that plagued us through the years was that the senior pastor's wife never got on board. A godly woman with many fine qualities, she just chose not to participate. The lack of her natural example, along with the years without a women's ministry staff presence, hindered our efforts the most. Woo your leadership's wives; share your vision with them and invite their participation. They are vital!

Build a Solid Relationship with the Staff Liaison

Many churches that have not yet added a woman on staff will provide the women's ministry with a liaison to the pastoral staff. Your relationship with him must thrive if your ministry is to succeed. Communication is key.

At our church, Liz communicated with our staff liaison at least once a month in a memo. We didn't include him in the day-to-day details or even the major decisions. We believed God gave women greater insight into the needs of other women. But we always explained our ideas clearly and asked his blessing before we proceeded. If he objected, we stopped. He always had good reasons, and we valued his counsel and direction.

Communicate the Exciting News

Because we ministered in a large church, we needed a way to communicate with all the women. In large churches, you may find your greatest challenge in communicating the upcoming launch. A pastoral announcement from the pulpit helps greatly—not only does every attendee hear it directly, but it acts as an official blessing from the church leadership. Paper handouts and email remain useful for updates. Pulpit announcements were rare in our church. Take advantage of the great number of social media and online tools to help spread the word about your ministry.

A SMALL CHURCH WITHOUT AN ORGANIZED WOMEN'S MINISTRY

I (Kelley) discovered Creekside Bible Fellowship as it celebrated its first-year anniversary. The congregation of ninety-plus people (including the growing nursery) had just begun renting space in a local business park. The façade of the young church resembled a plain white office building. Perhaps you are familiar with such a "store-front" church in your area. There are thousands across the nation.

Don't let small numbers discourage you from initiating a women's ministry. From the beginning, Creekside women held semester Bible studies and, within two years, had established an annual fall retreat. Wives of the pastor and elders were involved in this process, but they never ran the show exclusively. Over the years, we applied some of the principles found here, to great effect. The methods will look different for each small church, but the same end product is still the goal—a ministry that changes lives.

Bigger Isn't Better

Half of all American congregations list fewer than one hundred regularly participating adults.[21] Your resources may be limited, but God will furnish all you need. Don't sell yourself short just because your church isn't "mega." You'll enjoy unique advantages because of your intimate size.

The Same Principles Apply

You begin by selling your leadership on your vision. Write a proposal. Will they consider a woman on staff? Would your budget allow it? Maybe it is impossible now, but what about in the future? At Creekside, the long-range plan included a paid women's minister, when the right person came along and the church was able to pay her salary. In our eight years, we employed one women's director—on staff, but paid virtually nothing due to financial constraints. It worked for us for a while. Be flexible with your leadership and remember your goals. But plant the seed for such a director early, because sustaining quality and consistency without a woman on staff is difficult and frustrating. Be gracious. Assure your pastor you will work diligently whatever the resources.

Then enlist the women who show an interest in ministry to women in your church. Are there women who have taken the initiative to invite women into their homes? Is there an older woman the younger women go to for advice or encouragement? Does anyone distinguish herself as a woman who knows the Word? Are there professional women with skills in administration and leadership? Gather these women together to pray and brainstorm.

Do you know the demographics of your church? How many women are single, working, widowed, mothers of young children, etc.? In a small church, many of your women know one another. Is your church composed mainly of one group of women? That is more likely in a small church. Should you focus on ministry to them first?

You likely will find publicizing your new ministry easier in a small church. Will your pastor announce it from the pulpit? You don't have as much competition as in a larger church. Post flyers on the doors, stick them in the stalls of the restroom. Divide up your roster and make personal phone calls. What about a bulletin insert? A skit before a worship service? All of these methods worked for Creekside. Find out what works with your church.

Will your pastor's wife be involved? In a small church her absence is even more noticeable. Invite her graciously, but give her the freedom whether or not to participate according to her interests and other responsibilities. Don't expect her to teach the Bible or lead the ministry just because she married the pastor. Neither should she run the ministry from the sideline nor use her influence without discretion. Give her opportunities to serve with her unique gifts. Respect and protect her privacy. If she is part of the team, that will help your ministry. If not, don't resent her.

A Church with an Existing Women's Ministry

When I (Sue) was hired as pastor to women at Irving Bible Church, a healthy women's ministry was taking shape. Mary had been the women's ministry director for two years, although women's ministry existed long before she joined the staff. She brought a heart for women and expertise in events, but as much as she enjoyed ministry, her husband and two young sons needed her at home, so she made the decision to work part-time.

With our children grown, my husband and I believed God was calling me into full-time ministry. I came on staff to partner with Mary and to focus on building the Bible study. God paved the way for the transition.

Navigating Change

It wasn't easy for Mary to report to a newcomer. She was gracious, but I know that at times she found it difficult to watch me take the ministry in new directions. We differed in our gifts, personality, and leadership styles, but in many ways we complemented one another. I did not undo what was in place. I simply added to it. Nor did I try to change the way she worked. Fortunately, we melded as a team. Mary and I shared a common vision and model for ministry—the Transformation Model. And we were united in our commitment to both the postmodern and the modern women God sent us.

Mary had recruited influential women to serve and the pastor's wife supported us completely. Many of the initial steps were bypassed because of Mary's groundwork. I came on board in March and we were up and running with a new board and Bible study by September.

If You Encounter Resistance

Our experience was unusual. Often when a ministry already exists and newcomers appear with fresh ideas, conflict crops up. Often, women don't agree on the ministry model. In several denominations, older women are wedded to "modern" models that fit their generation but don't work with younger women now. Changing these denominational models means letting go of the past.

Some older women struggle to understand why these models don't work. They are easily wounded when younger women want to try a new model. How do you plant a new model against resistance? How do you honor women with different perspectives while not allowing them to dictate an outdated model?

First you confirm that you have your leadership's blessing. The pastor won't want women in the church feuding. Bring him a clear, written proposal of your vision, explain your reasoning, and assure him you want to work under his authority. If he agrees, move ahead. If he resists, this is not the time. God has other plans for you.

Next, connect with women you think may resist your efforts. Try not to see them as the enemy. One at a time, take them to lunch and share your ideas. When you pray over the meal, ask God to help you understand each other. Kindly inform them that the pastor knows and supports your vision. Ask for their ideas. If possible, include them in your plans. You may be surprised at the encouragement you receive. You may have to adjust some of your plans to win their support, but it will probably pay off long-term. If you can win these women over, the ministry will benefit.

If you cannot reconcile your views, hopefully you can agree to disagree. Can your ministries coexist side by side, giving women the choice of attending either or both? That may be your best option. If these women attempt to discredit you or your ministry, then you should follow the steps to healthy conflict resolution shared later in this section. Just be sure that you never say or do anything that might be perceived as criticism of their ministry. God will work it out over time.

If you have won them over or agreed to disagree, you are ready to begin. Gather women to pray. Visit other churches to observe their women's ministry. Read books on the subject. Follow the pattern already laid out in this section. Even though there is already a women's ministry in your church, in essence you are starting over.

In a Nutshell . . .

Whether God calls you to a large or small church, or a church with or without an existing women's ministry, the principles remain the same. You simply adjust them to your situation. In summary:

- Propose your dream to church leadership and receive their blessing and support.
- Meet with influential women in the church and share your vision.
- Enlist women with a heart for women to pray regularly with you for God's direction.
- Know your demographics so you can tailor-make your plans to their needs.
- Communicate the exciting news that you will soon launch!

How Northwest Bible Church First Hired a Women's Minister

"A key step in organizing a Women's Ministry program is to inform and educate the male leadership of the church, if they do not share the vision. It is a rare exception to find leadership that has a Women's Ministries program high on its agenda," writes Vickie Kraft, who served Northwest Bible Church in Dallas as women's minister for fourteen years.[22]

Here's how the women of her church hired Vickie.

> The women from Northwest Bible Church put together a written proposal. They included quotations from well-known women about the need for a relevant ministry to women and quotations from women in their own church in response to the survey. They detailed plans they had in mind. They demonstrated their conviction that a woman was needed on staff to administer the program. Then they invited the elders and their wives for dinner and presented each elder with a folder containing the program laid out clearly. They answered their questions and discussed the subject thoroughly. This thorough approach and the evidence the women offered convinced the elders, and, consequently, a salary for a minister to women was included in the next year's budget.[23]

Chapter 4

BUILD YOUR TEAM

Our goal is transforming women's lives. How does it happen? It trickles down from an inspired and passionate lead team!

We laughed until it hurt. We were celebrating the end of a fruitful year in women's ministries at our last board meeting. Our retreat chairperson arrived with a bright bag full of little wrapped boxes. Curiosity piqued, we asked, "What's in the boxes?"

"You'll see," she teased. After our meeting, she instructed us to take off our shoes and socks. Then she handed each of us a little box. We tore them open to find a toe ring inside each one.

Through the year we had chided her about her toe rings. She loved casual shoes and always revealed nicely pedicured toes sporting at least one toe ring. Somehow a woman in her late forties with toe rings made us laugh. We loved her young-at-heart attitude, her creativity, and her delight in exploring new ideas.

We slipped on our new toe rings and joined hands around the circle, women from twenty to sixty. We lifted our hearts in gratitude to a chorus of "I Love You, Lord." God had done great things! He had used this team to bring women to faith, grow them in his Word, and challenge them to serve.

As the women chatted, hugged, and laughed afterward, I thought back a year and a half earlier to when we had formed this team. Why had it worked? Certainly because God had blessed us. But we had also followed strategies that helped us connect and minister together. In this section, let's look at why teams are important (and biblical) and how to build an effective one.

WHY TEAMS?

Jesus built a team. In his three-year ministry on earth, he invested heavily in the Twelve. He chose them carefully and spent his days living with them as he trained them. He sent them out to minister in pairs. He taught them to work in groups. He knew when he founded his church that we are more productive together and that we need each other. He modeled team building, and that's reason enough for us to build them too. But we have observed that many women resist teams.

Do You Resist Teams?

Let's find out! Do you agree or disagree with these statements? Be honest!

- If I want something done right, I'd better do it myself.
- I'll have to set up meetings, and they are a waste of time.
- Most won't follow through and I'll have to do it all myself anyway.
- Teams ultimately mean conflict and I hate conflict.
- It takes more time to recruit a team than to do it all myself.
- I've had bad experiences with teams in the past.
- Teams are more trouble than they are worth.
- I don't want to be accountable for other people's mistakes.
- Why risk a team effort when I know I can meet the standards of excellence expected?
- I don't want to share the credit.

If you agreed with any of these statements, you may resist the team concept. We agree that, initially, building teams might take extra time. But if you refuse to invest in them, you'll pay a price. Teams are essential to the Transformation Model.

What's the Price?

When I observed a board member who wouldn't delegate, I started looking for a replacement. I did not have to ask her to leave. Inevitably, she'd burn out.

Laura expertly organized our women's dinners. She transformed the room into a showplace reflecting the theme of the dinner. It became a Hawaiian beach or a garden gazebo. The women knew it was the best ten dollars they would spend all year. But Laura refused to take the time up front to organize committees and call women who were eager to help.

As a result, she spent the last week alone hanging decorations from the ceiling and haggling with the caterer. Exhausted, she bailed out of her two-year commitment. Her replacement immediately implemented teams to help. The dinners ran with the efficiency of a German train, and the coordinator enjoyed the experience.

I grieved for Laura. God had given her extraordinary abilities to minister through these events. But her refusal to share the load took her down. You can carry the ministry by yourself for a while, but inevitably you'll burn out.

THE TRANSFORMATION MODEL REQUIRES TEAMS

The Transformation Model transforms women into mature, productive, joyful daughters of the King. For a woman to be transformed, she must have opportunities to see how God can use her. She must know her gifts and step out in faith expecting God to work through her. When she does, she experiences profound pleasure and usually surprise.

The feelings we experience when God works through us to teach and minister to women can't be described—only experienced. God wants every believer to know that joy! God expects leaders to offer multiple opportunities for women to serve.

OFFER MULTIPLE LEVELS OF
OPPORTUNITY IN ANY SIZE MINISTRY

1. Offer Entry-Level Opportunities

No matter what size your church, new believers and newcomers need entry-level opportunities to serve. These jobs will not sink your ministry if neglected. They don't require training, maturity, or expertise. In an entry-level job, you do not oversee others. Every ministry should divide the tasks in such a way that even new believers and women without experience can participate.

Do you provide service opportunities for women who have never volunteered before? Do you give newcomers a chance to show you who they are and what they can do? Are they nurtured by trained coordinators who will shepherd and instruct them so that they will enjoy a positive experience?

From these entry-level opportunities will bubble up women with leadership gifts. Women will emerge who are diligent, punctual, gifted, and personable. You will identify those who work well with others, those you can count on, and those who love women. One day, these women will lead the ministry. One day, one of them will sit where you sit.

That's the plan. Begin by using volunteers for entry-level tasks, but recruit women you know to serve as sub-team managers and coordinators.

2. Offer Sub-team Manager Positions

Once you have identified a woman who works well on a team and has the attitudes and gifts for overseeing others, give her a chance. For example, if you chair an event, let her be your registration coordinator. Find a woman with computer expertise and the gift of administration. Let her register women, oversee making name tags, and work the registration table. See how well she delegates. She might replace the coordinator next year.

In every area of ministry, these varied opportunity levels should be in place. The process of transformation cannot proceed without them.

3. Give Major Responsibilities to Tested Coordinators

The coordinator oversees the major facets of your ministry. She usually emerges by serving first at the entry and support levels. She has distinguished herself as a spiritually mature woman. She may be young in years, but is well grounded and shows promise. She works well on a team. She is passionate about her ministry. She understands the Transformation Model and knows that her work is more than accomplishing a task, putting on an event, or serving in a support capacity. She is building leaders with you, transforming women one at a time.

LET'S EXAMINE SOME TEAM-BUILDING PRINCIPLES

The Transformation Model is built on teams. To transform postmodern and modern women, we must embrace them one by one. You don't have enough arms or enough time to do that alone.

Refusing to work with others is often a sign that you fear losing control. Women's ministry is messy. It has been compared to herding cats. You may fear the conflict that might erupt when women work together. Maybe you've had a negative experience in the past that colors your perspective. Maybe you think you can do it better yourself. If your only concern is decorating the stage or providing a delicious dinner, you may pull it off. But that does not transform women's lives. To transform women requires multiple arms, hearts, and minds—and it's a lot more fun.

If teams scare you because you don't know how to build one, the following team-building principles should encourage you.

HOW WILL YOU STRUCTURE YOUR TEAM?

You can call your key leaders a team, board, committee, or anything you want. Make it fit your environment. It is important, however, that you give it a name—an identity. New millennium ministry may be characterized by *chaord,* but there is still order in *chaord,* and you'll need it to accomplish your vision.

STRUCTURE IN SMALL CHURCHES

Since the majority of churches in America average fewer than two hundred members,[24] most women's ministries won't need a large leadership team. But you *will* need a team. Guard against the tendency to do it all yourself because it is more expedient. However few women you have, the Transformation Model is about providing them opportunities to get involved and to develop their own potential for leadership in God's family.

I (Kelley) served on the women's leadership team at Creekside Bible Fellowship. The women's ministry averaged about twenty regular participants at this time, although that number spiked at our annual retreat. Our leadership structure fluctuated as well, but the most efficient team was made up of three, jokingly nicknamed "the Triumvirate."

The director of women's ministry served on a volunteer basis since the church plant could not afford her salary. Having previous experience and seminary training, the director wrote and taught the Bible studies, counseled women, and guided the vision of the ministry. She attended staff meetings and kept the male leadership informed about what the women were doing.

Depending upon the gifts and training of your director, she may wish to delegate some of these responsibilities to someone else under her management. For instance, she may recruit a teacher for the evening Bible study, a worship leader, someone to oversee childcare for the morning study, and someone to do hospitality. Effective directors delegate as much of the detail work as possible to other women. In doing so, she creates a sense of ownership and excitement in them as they serve other women.

The second member of our team, "the administrator," managed the women's finances, publicity, annual retreat, and various other details. With so many day-to-day responsibilities, the administrator of a small church's women's ministry is in a perfect position to form a small sub-team.

She might find someone who understands computer graphics to help with publicity. She would definitely want to recruit a retreat coordinator, hopefully someone who has experience with past retreats. With so few women involved, such helpers could make up the sub-team level of leadership rather than making each one a board position.

The "shepherd" held the third board position. She was responsible for the care of the women's souls. This meant practical as well as spiritual help. She saw that every hospitalized woman was visited, that meals were provided for new moms and the sick. She was there to disciple or coordinate others to disciple the women, so that each person would feel she had someone involved in her life who cared for her. It meant building relationships through the Bible study ministry so that she could more accurately assess where the women were spiritually. Although individual shepherding already occurred, this board position provided some accountability. It was a very pastoral role.

The women's leadership team provided a means for serving the women at Creekside, challenging them to greater responsibility and spiritual maturity. It did not always work perfectly, but the basic structure remained in place to keep the women's ministry on track even when our director resigned. Your church will not always experience straight paths and smooth waters, either. Be flexible, pray constantly, and work together.

STRUCTURE IN LARGE CHURCHES

The Makeup of a Leadership Team

What will your leadership team look like? Below, we will provide a thorough survey of your choices. Remember: depending upon your size and resources, some positions can be combined with others, some can be bypassed completely, and others can wait until the specific need arises. Take a look.

Team Leader

Someone must be in charge, whether she is paid staff or lay volunteer. The pastor to women or director of women's ministries (whatever you call her) is responsible for the overall ministry. Her duties may include overseeing the board, counseling, training women, and teaching the Bible study. She is also responsible for all events, the budget, and many other details. If you are blessed to have more than one woman on staff, there are many ways to divide up the responsibilities. Find a way that works for you.

Bible Study Coordinator

Design your working team to reflect the needs of your women. Begin with your ministry priorities. Remember: the Transformation Model is Bible study-centered. Therefore your first team position will probably be a Bible study coordinator.

How many Bible study coordinators will you need? If you plan more than one class, find a coordinator for each. How will you decide? If most of your women work, begin with a weekly Bible class that meets at night or on the weekend.

If there are just as many women who could attend during the day and you have the resources, begin with a night class *and* a day class. For moms with young children, provide childcare—first for the day class and later for the night class. Then your single moms can attend.

The Bible study coordinator runs the class. She recruits leaders and administrative teams to handle all the details. We will discuss Bible studies and the class coordinator's role in detail in later chapters.

Prayer Coordinator

Make prayer the foundation of your ministry. Every leader should include prayer in her work not only personally but also as part of the way she leads her team. A prayer coordinator may oversee prayer chains, special days of prayer, or prayer workshops. Her role is to promote prayer in the entire ministry. She should be a woman of prayer and passionate to help others pray. Knowing that prayer undergirds our women and our ministry encourages us all. Additionally, we attribute any ministry fruit to the power of prayer. Every ministry to women needs a prayer coordinator.

Administrative Secretary

This invaluable woman takes care of details. For example, the secretary is the communication link between the team leader and the team. She notifies members of meetings, changes, and procedures. She keeps minutes and records. She can also oversee the logistics, food, and transportation for team retreats and annual events that edify the team.

Event Coordinators

Although according to the Transformation Model, events are no longer central to women's ministry, women still love events. And they do offer value. Time away to focus on God and build relationships can have a profound effect on a woman's spiritual growth. These events often provide an entry point to propel women into other ongoing ministries. Events give women the chance to connect, relax, and laugh. Chapter 10 will show you how to create exciting events.

Identify events that benefit and appeal to women. Consider retreats, conferences for deep spiritual impact, light-hearted seminars, holiday dinners for fellowship and outreach, and whatever else your creative women dream up. You'll need a coordinator for each of your major events—like a weekend retreat. Some may be grouped depending on their complexity and timing.

The best event coordinators are strong administrators and encouragers. They sell their team on the vision of the event and then have fun getting prepared. Women who cannot commit to an ongoing ministry can often head up event teams.

Publicity Coordinator

Who informs the women and the church about your ministry? Who knows how to package what you do so that others will be excited about getting involved? The publicity coordinator's role depends on how much staff publicity support you enjoy. It also depends on the size of your church. This job in a large church looks different from the job in a small church.

In small churches, she may simply write bulletin announcements and design flyers for the halls or restroom stall doors. Publicity may be mostly word-of-mouth. She might make the women's ministry brochure on her computer or work with the church's technology team to keep the website current. With ready-to-order papers, attractive brochures can be produced that way.

If your church has in-house capabilities or supplies the budget, your publicity coordinator has the resources she needs. It may help, however, if she has experience in social media, graphic design, writing, and technology. Again, adapt this position to your setting.

Financial Coordinator

Who will handle the budget? I delighted to delegate the budget to a team member who excelled at numbers. I once recruited a young mother who was also a CPA. I am amazed at the number of professional women in our churches eager to use their accounting skills for the Lord.

Special Interests Coordinators

The larger your church, the more of these you will need. As your ministry establishes itself and you begin to branch out, special interest needs will emerge. Mothers of young children want a moms' ministry. Single moms have unique needs.

Divorcées and widows often request their own ministries—but don't group them together. Their circumstances and struggles differ, and they won't appreciate being linked. We will cover ministries for special groups in depth in chapter 11.

Missions Coordinator

Does your church prioritize missions? Do you want your women to enlarge their perspective and become global in their thinking? Are there opportunities for your women to actually take short-term mission trips? Can you find creative ways to encourage full-time missionaries sent out from your church?

A missions coordinator should be a woman with a heart for women all over the world and the ability to plan a ministry that will inspire others. The missions coordinator's goal is to promote a global perspective in all that your women do. We networked with our missions pastor and deliberately chose our missions coordinator from women on the church-wide missions team. That way we were assured of working together. This position looks different depending on the way your church handles missions. Again, complement what already exists in the church.

At my former church, we labeled this position *outreach* and asked the coordinator to oversee both inner-city and world missions. We structured the position this way because missions were done through the denomination and there was limited access to full-time missionaries. Few short-term mission trips were planned through the church. Every church does missions differently. Assess yours and complement it.

Mercy Ministry Coordinator

Many women's ministries include some form of mercy ministry. This can take two forms: helping the needy within your church body, then perhaps reaching out to those outside the church. First, design a ministry to meet the needs in your own body. At IBC we called it *Many Hands.*

Many Hands volunteers took meals and cleaned homes of the sick, visited those in need of encouragement, did handyman jobs, provided transportation, and met other special needs. It began in women's ministry and expanded churchwide.

Second, we also supported a food pantry by collecting food monthly from our Bible studies. The coordinator recruited volunteers and stayed abreast of the needs within the church congregation.

Affirmation Coordinator

Hebrews 3:13 commands us to "encourage one another daily." As the team leader, you may not have sufficient time and energy to show your appreciation to the team members and volunteers. Find a woman with the gift of encouragement, give her a budget, and unleash her.

Our affirmation coordinator made sure everyone felt appreciated, and she planned a special dinner for the lead team in late spring. She hosted dinners for our Bible study leaders and coleaders twice a year. She found unique ways to say thank you and modeled the gracious spirit of a grateful woman.

Hospitality Coordinator

If your board wants help with food, recruit a hospitality coordinator. Find a woman who knows food and caterers, who loves to oversee its preparation and make it look good, and who enjoys assisting others. She helps with dinners, lunches, and our team kickoff retreat. If it involves food, she's the resource.

Historian

We want our memories recorded. The method depends on your church. At IBC, we highlighted events of the past through a year-end video. These days social media and a website may provide all you need. A creative woman will thrive in this role. Equip her with resources and enjoy the labor of her hands and heart.

WHAT POSITIONS SHOULD YOU INCLUDE ON YOUR TEAM?

Look over the list and choose what fits your vision and resources. There may be some not on this list or you may call them by different names. Make it work for you. If you are just getting started, keep it small. Small churches wisely limit what they do to what they can do well. If you have four widows, don't organize a widow's ministry. They should be able to link up without it.

At a minimum, include a team leader and her assistant, and coordinators for Bible study, prayer, and events. Then perhaps choose a secretary, publicity coordinator, and financial coordinator, or find someone who can do all three tasks. If needed, others can be added in time.

Don't forget to add your Bible teachers to your team if they are not already involved. They are leaders in your ministry and should be included. In addition, they will be better teachers if they understand the heartbeat of the ministry and cooperate with you.

WHICH ARE SUPPORT POSITIONS?

As you recruit your team, consider that some of your leaders will need to recruit their own teams to carry out their ministry—but others won't. These are support positions and can usually be accomplished solo. As a result, the women who serve in support capacities won't need team-building skills. Support positions include secretary, publicity, finances, affirmation, and historian. These women may get help but won't absolutely need it to do a good job.

How Long Should a Team Member Serve?

We recommend term limits for lead team members with a few exceptions. If you don't limit the time board members serve, you will be perceived as clannish and cliquish. In the Transformation Model, you want to give as many women as possible the chance to develop their gifts and have the opportunity to experience God working through them.

The exceptions would be staff positions and unique ministries that are too extensive for a lay leader to be expected to tackle. For example, the standard of excellence at our retreat made it unreasonable to ask a new volunteer to head it up. The same woman led IBC's retreat for twenty years before handing it off to her assistant. These lay volunteers were so exceptional that we allowed them to remain on the board. No one objected.

But under ordinary circumstances and for the health of your ministry, limit the time your team serves. We asked our women to commit to two years with a third-year option. At the beginning of the third year, we discussed whether a third year was recommended. Three years works very well for women working with sub-teams. For example, our Bible study coordinators learned the job the first year, fine-tuned it the second, and trained their replacement the third.

When considering the third-year option, we looked at personal circumstances, the health of the ministry, and the individual woman's desires. If she wanted to serve a third year and it worked for her family and the ministry, we were delighted.

An ideal scenario sees about half your team rolling off each year. The seasoned members set the tone for the year as they welcome and train newcomers. This has occurred naturally with the teams I have planted. Some women move away. Others won't delegate and burn out. Some take the two-year option because of personal circumstances.

How Do You Recruit Your Team?

First, write clear job descriptions. See Appendix A for samples. Ask each team member to rework these every year to reflect what she is actually doing.

Then meet with several women leaders or your entire team to pray and brainstorm possibilities. Your team members often know just the right women to replace them. Try to come up with several women for each open position.

Consider their gifts, age, and experience. Try to balance your board so that a variety of women bring differing perspectives. I tried to recruit several young single women if possible. I wanted a young mom and some older women. Ideally the team should reflect the makeup of your ministry.

For key leadership positions, choose women that you know well. One wrong choice can make a miserable year. Be selective. If God doesn't bring someone to mind, wait.

Recruiting Your First Lead Team

Recruiting your first team is a bit different. You may not know the women that well. Move ahead despite the risk. The first year we put together a lead team at my former church, we made two or three terrible choices. We had no experience working with these women so we chose the ones who appeared to be most qualified. They weren't always the best choices, but we learned over time.

The Recruiting Process

The woman who oversees the entire ministry should do the recruiting. The team works for you and needs to know that from the start.

If you are just getting started or the board is small, you may want to meet face-to-face with each candidate. Otherwise phoning them is fine. Before you begin your calls, pray that God will give these women discernment. You don't want them to say "yes" unless they are led by God. You don't want over-committed or status-seeking women. You want women who are passionate about serving women and glorifying God.

Next, examine your list. Which board position is most strategic to next year's ministry? Which suggestion is the strongest? Often the same woman may be suggested for several positions. Where do you need her most? Ask her about that position first.

When you reach her, tell her that you would like for her to pray about serving on the board next year. Ask her if this is a possibility. If she knows up front that she is moving or is already too busy, then you both save time. If she says she will consider it, then proceed.

Describe the position you have in mind and ask if she thinks this might be a fit for her gifts and passion. If that job is not a good fit, you might suggest another position. If she is open, explain the details.

A Suggested Checklist

- Send her the job description.
- Suggest that she dialogue with the outgoing team member.
- Inform her of everything else expected. Tell her when the team meetings are scheduled.
- Give her the date of the team's kickoff training retreat and explain that her attendance is mandatory.
- Explain that she will be working as part of a team and that her input and prayer support are vital to the success of the ministry.
- If your team is required to attend one of your weekly Bible studies, make sure she understands that requirement.
- Explain the two-year commitment with a possible third.
- Tell her she would be serving with an incredible team doing God's work in women's lives—and that she'll have fun!
- If she is still interested, ask her to pray for at least a week and discuss this with family members.

Then wait for her answer. Don't call someone else for this position until you hear from her, but continue down your list until you have asked someone to fill each position. A week later, call each one back. If she accepts, express your delight and explain when her term begins. If she declines, thank her for wisdom in listening to God's leading. Then call the next woman on the list.

Recruiting goes in rounds and may take a couple of hours once a week for several weeks. Begin to recruit several months before your new team begins its term. Women usually plan their year in advance and they are often already committed if you wait until later. The longer your ministry is established and the more fruit it produces, the easier it is to recruit your team. Women want to be a part of an exciting women's ministry!

How Long Should a Lay
Minister Serve without Pay?

If the church won't or can't pay you, how long should you serve as director in a volunteer capacity? A director or minister who serves only a limited term of a couple of years adversely affects the ministry. In most circumstances, asking a woman to work staff hours indefinitely without pay is unreasonable. Asking her to do the work of the ministry without the benefit of networking with other staff causes all the women to feel slighted.

Let's consider the issue. Ministry to women is one of the last ministry frontiers. As a result, many churches do not understand the value of having a woman on staff to shepherd their women. In some churches, tradition bars the door. In small churches, the leaders may see the value but money is the limiting factor. But because of Titus 2 and the fact that over half of most churches are female, women need a female shepherd. Without consistent leadership, any ministry will flounder. What can you do? Here are some options:

If Your Church Can Afford It, Ask Your Leaders for a Woman on Staff

In chapter 3, we told you about how the women of Northwest Bible Church sought approval for a women's minister on staff to lead them. They not only wrote a proposal, they served their leaders a delicious dinner. Then they presented them with a folder detailing their vision and hopes. They presented their request graciously and also asked to be a part of the search process. Their efforts resulted in Vickie Kraft and fourteen years of a model ministry that has impacted other churches around the world. This is the best result for the health of the ministry.

Stay and Serve without Pay

If you are financially able, you can stay and serve, hoping that in time the leadership will recognize the value of your work. I did this for seven years at an earlier church. We poured our hearts into the women, and I loved it. I admit I longed to be part of the staff, but the ministry was enough. However, I could have been more effective as a bona fide member of the team. In addition, the church would have benefited from a woman's perspective on the leadership team.

Sometimes it was humorous. Secretaries throughout the church would alert us when the church forgot us in a brochure or ministry fair. We would find a gracious way to remind the leadership that we existed. They didn't exclude us intentionally—we simply were not part of the tradition. Nevertheless, it was hard to feel that the leaders really valued women.

I delight in the knowledge that we did not strive in vain: soon after my time there ended, the leadership did put a woman on staff as director of women's ministries.

Ask to Be Part of the Staff with Little or No Pay

If you know your church budget definitely can't afford you and you don't need the money, you might consider asking to serve on staff with very little or no pay. Maybe you could be half- or quarter-time. Of course you would probably log more hours, but at least you would be participating with the staff. As the church was able, they could increase your pay.

While not a very good option, this strategy provides some advantages. You bring consistency to women's ministry by serving longer than two years. In my experience, replacing directors every few years brings trouble. Consistent vision and momentum is lost. It takes time for women to trust the leader.

Leave, Trusting God Has a Better Place

If you need the money or find you cannot work a staff member's hours as a volunteer with a good heart attitude, then you need to leave. Your anger or resentment will never honor God. Trust him to lead you to the right place for you.

Your women's ministry will never flourish if you change directors like light bulbs. But church leaders are accountable to God for the spiritual health of their women. Do all you can without an angry heart or rebellious attitude. Then trust God—he is faithful.

Chapter 5

RALLY YOUR TEAM

And let us consider how we may spur one another on toward love and good deeds, not giving up meeting together, as some are in the habit of doing, but encouraging one another—and all the more as you see the Day approaching.

—Hebrews 10:24–25

"The most effective churches today develop team-based leadership. This pattern will likely continue into the twenty-first century, both because Scripture emphasizes Spirit-led, Spirit-gifted, collaborative team fellowship and because today's culture is receptive to such leadership," writes team expert George Cladis.[25]

WHY SHOULD YOUR TEAM MEET?

If a woman questions the need for your team to meet periodically, you can bet she is not a team player. We meet because God's work benefits. We meet because we all benefit. When the team gathers, each member understands that she serves as part of the whole of what God is doing. She is less likely to become territorial and shortsighted. Our gatherings produce energy and momentum as we hear about God's movement in other facets of the ministry. If we are discouraged, we pray for one another and help one another with new ideas. If we are fruitful, we rejoice together.

If you desire to minister to postmoderns as well as moderns, you will need them on your teams. Young women are not content to sit on the sidelines. Involve them or lose them.

How Often Should Your Team Meet?

Meetings are beneficial—but nobody likes unnecessary meetings. Women are busy. Don't meet when you don't need to. When I led IBC's women, our team met seven times a year. We scheduled our meetings a year in advance in order to get on everyone's calendar early.

We chose a regular meeting day and time and met during the evening so working women could participate. While the majority of the board preferred daytime meetings, they were willing to come in the evening because they understood the importance of including the single and working women.

Even when we planned a year ahead, last-minute emergencies and responsibilities kept our team from attending every meeting. This sort of thing will happen no matter how much your team members want to be there. Nevertheless, it is your assignment to make the meetings something no one wants to miss.

How Do You Run a Team Meeting That No One Wants to Miss?

Make every minute meaningful. These gatherings should be informal, fun, and inspiring—you aren't leading a plumbing supply budget meeting. Use this time to evaluate your ministry in light of your vision statement, encourage one another, and hear the great things God is doing. Get feedback and come to the aid of anyone struggling. Establish some ground rules, such as:

- **Limit your meeting length to two hours.**

- **Prepare an agenda.**
  The agenda shows you have a well-thought-out plan. Follow the agenda unless a good reason exists to be flexible. The flow of a typical meeting includes elements like prayer, a devotional, or an informative report about a new ministry. Give every leader who wants to an opportunity to communicate what's happening in her arena.

- **No two-party business allowed.**
  That means that we don't waste time discussing what could better be hammered out by the two people involved. Team meetings are not the time to discuss details anyway, and the leader should make that clear.

- **Don't do all the talking.**
  Interaction adds interest. Encourage everyone to participate. Make your ministry relational, suggests George Cladis:

Relational ministry best sums up the ministry of Jesus. God did not send a committee or an organization to die on the cross for us. God sent his Son who loves us, teaches us, rebukes us, redeems us, and empowers us—all very relational dynamics! Ministry teams that are relational and network forming rather than bureaucratic have wonderful opportunities to grow and thrive in the postmodern world.[26]

- **Challenge the team to grow.**
  Consider implementing active learning exercises, team-building challenges, and spiritual growth opportunities.

  We usually began our meetings with a devotional from one of the members. The first-year women shared their stories. Sometimes I assigned a book to read and discuss.

  You may want to include a training section in each meeting, especially if your team is full of women new to ministry. Be creative and don't be afraid to ask your team to do reasonable assignments that will help them.

- **Emphasize prayer requests and prayer for one another.**
  You can let your prayer coordinator oversee this part of the meeting. Always begin with a short prayer if you do business first. Prayer sets the tone and reminds everyone that we are about God's work. Personal and ministry prayer requests are appropriate.

  Connecting as people is just as important as doing business. We loved one another and wished to hear about one another's lives. Emphasize confidentiality. If time was limited we often paired off and prayed for one another. Don't neglect prayer. You are modeling the principle that this is God's ministry.

- **Listen respectfully to everyone's ideas.**
  Provide a safe atmosphere where the team can suggest ideas and

never fear humiliation. When you ask for input, you may occasionally get some unusual responses. While you would never consider implementing every suggestion, especially the unwise ones, neither do you want to discourage any woman from participating. Often as you brainstorm, a good idea grows out of a bad idea. Respectfully listen to even the newest and untrained member.

- **Don't be negative or critical.**
  When women arrive late or don't follow through, it is easy to be negative. If team members aren't faithful, you may feel like reprimanding them at the meeting. Don't! This is not the time. Do this privately and gently, assuring the women that you have their best interests in mind and that of the ministry as a priority. If board members are in conflict, address the issue privately as well.

  You set the tone for the meeting. If you are negative, they will be negative. And discouragement will take you all spiraling down. Discuss general problems with an upbeat attitude that shows you trust God to help and overcome.

- **Set the atmosphere for maximum effect.**
  Be sure the environment enhances your meeting. This is important wherever ministry happens. Consider how many people attend. At Creekside, we usually had about six. At IBC, we expected between ten and fifteen. Consider holding your meetings in a cozy, intimate room. We set up the tables in a U or a circle so everyone saw everyone else. Our secretary or hospitality coordinator made sure coffee, tea, and goodies were available. We dressed casually. We laughed and usually hung around afterward just because we enjoy being together. And we did our two-party business then.

Atmosphere matters! Cladis, in his book *Leading the Team-Based Church,* says,

Years ago I was sent by my denomination to report to a session about the work of the denomination. The pastor and his clerk sat at a head table. The twenty-four elders present sat in chairs that faced the head table. . . . All eyes were on the pastor-moderator who led the discussion and answered most of the questions raised. He was set up as the authority and the one responsible for the organization, the one with all the answers. Configuration speaks volumes. Change it to reflect an enabling style. Meet in a circle. Although the moderator is certainly a principal player . . . spread out power and responsibility so that more and more people are the answer-tellers.[27]

Plan your team gatherings prayerfully and carefully. What happens there trickles down and impacts everything else you do. When your lead team enjoys encouragement, prayer support, financial resources, and training, it will partner with God to transform women's lives!

How Do You Transition from the Old Team to the New Team?

Each year about half our team were newcomers. Some didn't know anyone on the board well. How did we help them feel included and unleash them for ministry? We needed an extended time together to share the vision, to hear their stories, to bond them with other members, and to equip them for their calling.

IBC's lead team took two days away in early summer to transition in the new board. In addition, we needed a block of time to evaluate the past year and to pray and plan for the year ahead. We left town to limit distractions. Church members lent us their lake or ranch houses for this concentrated weekend.

We used to call this our team *retreat* but it was so labor-intensive, the team teased me about false advertising. We changed it to *training camp* and invited those who wanted time to actually relax to come a day before or stay after. We had so much to accomplish during those two days that we packed nearly every minute with stuff to do.

But don't forget to balance the intense times with times to relax and enjoy each other. Include an evening of informal games even for those who don't attend the extra day. If you are as task-oriented as I am, you need a reminder not to schedule every second. Down times are valuable too.

What did we do during training camp? We chose a theme for the weekend by asking God to show us the board's greatest need for the year ahead. One year our Bible studies exploded with new women. A major emphasis that year was acclimating all those women. We wanted to sensitize our team and their volunteers to how it felt to be new.

A sample schedule for the team training camp weekend:

FRIDAY

8:30 A.M.	Leave the church
10:30 A.M.	Arrive, unpack
11:00 A.M.	Gather for preview of weekend

- Play "Bafa Bafa"—a game where the women divide up and create two different cultures, with opportunities to interact as a newcomer to the other culture.
- Discuss results.

12:30 P.M.	Lunch and break
2:00 P.M.	Gather for story time

- The new women pass a three-minute egg timer and tell everything they can about themselves in three minutes.

2:30 P.M.	Training on characteristics of postmodern women

- Discussion on how to include them and retain older women
- Ten-minute break at 3:30

4:30 P.M.	Tell more stories

- Returning members pass the egg timer.

5:00 P.M.	Praise and worship

- Members share one-sentence blessings.
- Praise songs led by our arts coordinator

5:30 P.M.	Prepare and eat dinner
7:00 P.M.	Games and fun

- If women don't know each other well, plan fun activities to bond them.

SATURDAY

8:30 A.M.	Breakfast
9:30 A.M.	Team reports

- Each member reviews the year and shares vision for

	the next year, handing out a one-page report that she prepared ahead.
	• Ten-minute break at 10:30
11:00 A.M.	Business (procedures, rosters, explain and sign conflict resolution contract, etc.)
11:30 A.M.	Old board member meets with new board member to hand over materials and to discuss the ministry.
12:30 P.M.	Lunch
1:30 P.M.	Gather to take prayer requests, both personal and ministry-related.
3:00 P.M.	Prayer, commissioning, communion
4:00 P.M.	Pack and drive home

Make your training camp fit your ministry. Remember: these two days are invaluable! They equal the time you will spend in board meetings for the rest of the year. If you forfeit this initial time together, you probably will not experience the depth in relationships that fosters ministry success. If two days away won't work for you, find other blocks of time together before or early in the ministry year. The fruit you experience throughout every other facet of your ministry begins here.

How Do You Schedule a Last-Minute Meeting?

Occasionally, you will need to schedule an emergency meeting. Or perhaps one team member cannot physically attend. Technology can be your best friend in these situations.

While the names of the tools will change over time, and more will come along, we have found a tool like Doodle (www.doodle.com) invaluable. It helps you determine times and dates everyone can gather, in person or online.

Determine which online organizational tools your team will use to enhance communication and efficiency, such as Google calendar, Outlook, Zoom, FaceTime, Skype, etc.

Build trust and have fun. Again we turn to Cladis:

> Leadership teams that build trust are teams that spend time together. There is no substitute for this time together. Trust is

dependent upon a narrative of events that builds up the team's identity and confidence. Those events will be both serious and playful. The serious events will be the ones in which the team worked through crisis and brutally honest sharing. The playful events will be the ones in which the team learned about one another's gifts, personalities, and approaches to life.[28]

Invest and enjoy!

Chapter 6

CREATE YOUR OWN LIFE-CHANGING BIBLE STUDIES

Ashley clicked off her e-mail after a quick reply to her boss. Work followed her everywhere. Four-year-old Erin pulled on her arm. "Can I have mac and cheese for dinner—pleeeeeze?" Ashley poked holes in the plastic, popped the tray in the microwave, and pondered the evening's plans as she waited.

She had promised her coworker Susan that she'd go to church with her tonight. *Why did I do that?* She knew why. Susan was a real friend—the mom Ashley never had. And although some of Susan's ideas were strange, Susan was always there for her. She would go for Susan—just this once.

She felt guilty leaving Erin another night. But at least she'd kept Erin. Maybe Jerry would watch her tonight? Jerry arrived as Ashley finished putting on Erin's coat.

"Can she stay home with you? I rented a video. Couldn't you two just hang out?"

"Sorry, I've got too much work to do."

Oh well, she wasn't Jerry's kid anyway. Susan said they had stuff for kids to do. Maybe Erin would have fun. Susan honked and they piled in. They talked work on the way with Susan doing more talking than usual.

As they pulled into the parking lot, Ashley observed every kind of woman emerge from the cars—women in pant suits with briefcases, mothers towing toddlers, women in sweats, silver-haired grandmothers, and teenagers. Some were loud as they greeted each other from across the parking lot. Others hugged. *This could be really weird,* thought Ashley.

They walked briskly through doors held open by smiling women. One hugged Susan, then asked about her grown son Ben. After news about Ben, the woman reached out her hand to Ashley. "Who's this?" she asked. Susan introduced her. The woman looked in her eyes and said, "Good to meet you. Hope you enjoy yourself tonight." She seemed to mean it.

They left Erin with a woman in "Kids Klub" and they were off again, swept along in a current of women. The room was bigger than any church Ashley had ever been in. It was full of round tables, spaced out into every nook. As they whisked by tables, she saw that some had lit candles and others had flowers floating in shallow vases. All had food—trays of vegetables, or chips and dips, or sweets. They looked homemade.

There must have been twenty-five or thirty tables. As they passed a doorway, she noticed more tables outside in a foyer. And she smelled something delicious out there. Susan suggested that after they settled in she get them a latte or cappuccino from the coffee bar. *A coffee bar in a church! This is a strange place.*

When they reached their table, Susan introduced Ashley to their leader and the women chatting around the table. Two stopped their conversation and greeted her. Ashley sat down while Susan went for cappuccinos.

Then a frightening reality hit Ashley. In a few minutes, this table was going to fill with women. And when it did they would sit face to face. What did they expect from her?

They all had Bibles and notebooks. Ashley didn't own a Bible. What were they going to talk about—religious stuff? She would have nothing to say. Then again, she did watch Oprah when she was home sick.

Someone was talking over the mike. She looked up, and on the stage a little white-haired woman beamed. "Welcome. I'm Barb. Please find your seats and we will get started." She paused for a minute as women scurried to their places, and then she prayed, "Dear Father, we gather tonight to learn more about you and to encourage one another. Help us understand your truth. Help us live it out. We love you. In Jesus's name. Amen."

Jackie, a curly-headed woman in her thirties, bounded onto the platform and directed their attention to large screens, one on each side of the stage. On each screen was a painting of the ocean with giant waves catapulting against rock cliffs. "Tonight, Philippians will teach us how to have joy in the midst of tough times. Look at this painting. Even though the waves swell to fifty feet on the surface, fifty feet underneath the ocean floor is peaceful and calm.

"The waves are the circumstances in our lives. We can't control them and often they toss us about until we think we will go under. But even as we are tossed about, deep within us, God can give us a peace that passes all understanding. Tonight we will learn about that peace and how to possess it."

Then her tone changed. She grinned, "I know some of you just came from a long day at work and you could use a back rub. So let's all turn to the person on our right and give each other a little massage. And then when you're done, look under your chair. If you find a green dot, you are the winner of a full body massage." After a short back rub, everyone scrambled. Soon the winner ran up front with the green dot on her finger to claim her prize. Ashley's brow lifted. *A church that gives away massages! Now I've seen everything.*

The women sat down around the tables. Ashley didn't pull her chair up close to the table like the other women—not until later. Susan introduced Ashley to the group, explaining that she often helped her on computer projects that were beyond her expertise. She praised Ashley's attempts to be a good mother to Erin. Susan seemed to understand and appreciate Ashley's desire to rebuild her life. Ashley felt warm inside.

Their leader asked the women if there were any prayer requests. They began to write them on note cards and hand them to the leader. A prayer request? What would she write? Then she remembered that Erin's day care was closing and she needed to find another caregiver while she worked. She wrote that on her card.

The leader read each request and a few women elaborated. They had real problems. One's marriage was in trouble. At least they were married. She wondered if Jerry would ever suggest marriage. Another's mom had cancer. Her mammogram had uncovered a lump and she was going for a biopsy tomorrow. One was trying to quit smoking.

The leader took the cards and laid them in the center of the table. Susan whispered to her that they use the cards to pray later, but no one would pressure her to pray out loud. *Good!*

The table leader led them in a discussion of Bible study questions they had answered at home. There were three levels of questions, so they could do as little or as much study as they wanted during the week. As Susan handed Ashley a Bible, the leader commented, "Don't feel any pressure to participate, Ashley. I know all this is new. Just sit back and enjoy." *Whew!* What followed was a respectful, honest, in-depth exchange of opinions and perspectives on the Bible passage. Ashley listened intently. The women didn't always agree, but they were kind to each other.

Susan looked up the passage in Philippians for Ashley to follow along as the group shared what the passage meant to them—and they talked personal stuff. She didn't know if she would ever have the courage to unmask herself that way.

That little white-haired Barb's voice came over the speakers again. Time to close down the discussion. Time to hear about opportunities to learn more and serve others. The leader passed out a paper listing the times, places, and people who needed this and that—inner-city ministry, a mission trip to Russia, an upcoming MOMs ministry meeting. They passed around a list to sign if you were interested in workplace ministry and another list if you could bring canned goods for the food pantry.

Suddenly the room darkened. A quick video pictured two women sitting on a couch consoling one another. Their father had died and they were helping one another cope. Ashley identified with one of the sisters. She had felt that way when her father died six years earlier. Tears filled her eyes as she heard the women on the video articulate feelings she'd buried. She wiped them away quickly as the lights came up.

The spotlight shifted to Sara, the teacher. The coleader passed out an outline of her message. Sara talked about her years before Christ. She pointed to her hip and revealed that there was a little devil tattooed there. She related the heartache of those days—part of that she brought on herself. Then she talked about struggles now.

She said to expect these hard times—they were part of life. She drew principles out of the Bible passage they discussed at the table and showed how these principles could work in life today.

Ashley took notes on her phone and wrote down several Bible quotes she especially wanted to remember. The teacher used a movie clip to illustrate a truth. Ashley was familiar with the movie, and what the teacher said made sense. The teacher's voice was strong but full of love. Her words rang true. *Maybe the Bible isn't a book of myths and fairy tales.*

For her last illustration, the teacher explained that sometimes our joy must come from what is ahead. For the Christian that meant looking forward to being with Christ in eternity.

Sara told the story of a woman who knew she was going to die. She invited her pastor to her home to plan her funeral.

"I want to be buried with a fork in my hand," the woman insisted.

When the pastor asked why, she explained, "At potluck dinners, after we eat the main course, someone always says, 'Keep your fork.' That means that dessert is coming—chocolate velvet pie and lemon squares and brownies. That is always the best part. I want to be buried with a fork in my hand to let people know that the best is yet to come."

When Sara finished her story, the coleaders passed around a plastic golden fork for everyone to take home. It was wrapped with a gold and silver bow and a card with Romans 8:28, "And we know that in all things God works for the good of those who love him, who have been called according to his purpose." *Could that be true?* Ashley slipped the gold fork into her purse.

After the message, the table drew back together for a "concert of prayer." Women who wanted to pray aloud took a card from the requests in the center of the table. The leader again soothed Ashley's fears by telling the whole table there was no pressure to pray out loud. But most of them did.

Someone prayed for Erin. They prayed that God would lead Ashley to a caretaker where Erin would be safe and nurtured. Ashley could hear muffled voices from all over the room seeking God's best for their sisters.

A leader closed prayer time by playing softly on the piano, and then everyone joined in a chorus that centered on joy—a supernatural, abundant joy that comes only from God. Ashley sang along, a song that came from somewhere deep within her. A closing prayer. A room of laughter and conversation.

Susan and Ashley picked up a cheery Erin who had made a friend who wanted her to come over and play next Saturday. Ashley was quiet during the ride home. Her journey had begun.

Ashley's story represents the ideal. In reality the woman at the door may have forgotten to greet Ashley or a child may have hurt Erin's feelings in Kids Klub. But despite the occasional blunder, this format worked at IBC. In fourteen years we tripled our attendance. Every year we tweaked the study to heighten our effectiveness.

What kind of a Bible study will transform the postmodern and modern women God sends you? This chapter will help you design and implement just the right Bible study for your women.

Why Is Bible Study the Priority?

What will change Ashley's life? What will transform her into a joyful woman of integrity and strength? Only one thing. She must experience an intimate relationship with Jesus. And that relationship begins and grows as she interacts with his Word.

After you establish the lead team, your next priority is Bible study. Remember, churches with flourishing ministries to women center around Bible study. The size of a church or the number of women involved has no bearing on this principle.

The Scriptures are God's love letters to his children. They convey his heart and mind, and they are the primary way God communicates with us. God expects us to understand his Word thoroughly and to apply it diligently. Through understanding the Bible, we learn to know and love God intimately. And when we do, we are transformed!

What happens behind the scenes to make possible such change in women's lives? How will you create an experience that will propel them deep into God's Word? Whether you minister in a large or small church, pursue the same goal—to partner with God to take them deep into the Bible as he transforms your women.

Effective women's ministries must make the Bible their priority, but each will use different methods. How will you structure your study for maximum impact? What resources are available? Tailor your structure to the needs of your women. Investigate other women's ministries for ideas, but don't merely duplicate. What works for them may not work for you. Gather your team and pray. Then hammer out answers to the following questions.

Will You Study Books *of* the Bible or Books *on* the Bible?

First, you must decide *what* you will study. Will it be in-depth studies that guide your women through a book of the Bible like Genesis or the Gospel of Luke? Will you dig into studies with biblical themes like the covenants or the parables of Jesus? Or will you serve up studies on topics like forgiveness and friendship or the hot bestseller on how to live for Christ? All are valuable—but which will transform your women with more power and impact? We recommend a steady diet of books of the Bible or biblical themes with sporadic snacks of topical studies. Why?

> A person has deprived himself of the best there is in the world who has deprived himself of a knowledge of the Bible. . . . There are a good many problems before the American people today, and before me as president, but I expect to find the solutions of these problems in just the proportion that I am faithful in the study of God's Word. I beg you, read it. Find out for yourselves that the Bible is the Word of life. Read, not little snatches here and there, but long passages that will be the road to the heart of it.[29]

The Bible contains sixty-six separate documents written over a period of more than fourteen hundred years by more than forty human authors from varied cultures. Yet it is a single unit. Each book is interwoven with the others, fitting together to produce the only literary work in history without error. God, inspiring and empowering human authors, gave us a living book with the power to transform us supernaturally from the inside out. Study it to better understand the character of God and truths related to the world, and for the purpose of life change, not just head knowledge.

Topical studies of particular interest to women provide a nice change of pace. Consider using topical studies as a summer alternative when schedules change and attendance can be inconsistent. Online retailers and Christian bookstores stock many options by reputable Bible teachers.

But topical studies usually focus on pertinent Bible verses, often plucked out of context. Without understanding the context, readers more likely misunderstand and misinterpret the full meaning of cited passages. In their favor, these studies are easy to organize. Order a booklet for each participant, recruit a group leader, and enjoy digging into a topic together. However, your core curriculum should focus on books or themes in the Bible because they change lives. Studying the Bible itself, instead of books about the

Bible, does require more effort on the part of the leaders. One of you must know the Bible in order to guide others. You must find a curriculum that fits your needs or recruit someone with the biblical and writing expertise to create your own studies. Some controversial passages can stir up theological disagreements that you will need to research and address.

The Bible is not always easy to understand. Reading ancient literature can sometimes seem like hunting buried treasure. You need to know the historical and cultural background as well as geography. Untangling detailed passages will frustrate lazy women. Avoid the temptation to choose topical or studies on popular books because they are simpler to understand.

It is worth the extra effort to bring your women deep into the heart of God's Word by tackling whole books of the Bible. Longtime pastor and author Andy McQuitty offers some benefits.

> You can take virtually any book of the Bible, Old or New Testament, and teach through it expositionally and you will find occasion to teach on every felt need. . . . You've got to have confidence that God's Word is sufficient to touch the needs of your people.
>
> It's important as teachers of God's Word that we are forced to deal with passages that we wouldn't necessarily choose. First, we need to not let our teaching ministry be guided by our personal preferences. We're supposed to teach the whole counsel of God's Word. . . . The second benefit is for your students. They encounter passages that seem inconsistent, harsh or confusing. If their spiritual leaders are only teaching the popular, the passionate, the easy passages and are skirting around the difficult ones, it may create in the minds of students an insecurity that maybe there is no way to understand or reconcile the difficult passages. So we actually diminish our students' confidence in the Word of God because we don't deal with tough things. Expository teaching forces us to deal with issues that ultimately strengthen students.[30]

If you want to transform women, use the most powerful tool available. Study God's Love Letter, the Bible.

WILL YOU WRITE YOUR OWN STUDIES OR BORROW FROM THE "EXPERTS"?

Writing a quality Bible study takes a lot of time, as well as biblical and writing expertise. If you are limited on time or resources, you can buy excellent Bible studies written by gifted scholars and teachers. Check out their credentials and be sure you and/or your team evaluate the study by working through it thoroughly before you serve it to your women.

If you want to create your own material, recruit writers in your flock who have the ability, time, and desire to write studies especially for the women you shepherd. Or if you enjoy writing and have been adequately trained in your understanding of the Scriptures, you may want to take on this task yourself. But be sure you have margin in your schedule. There's no shame in using others' curriculum as long as you vet it well.

Sue's Experience

In the parachurch Bible study where I was trained, the leaders always wrote their own Bible studies. I would never have tried to write my own lessons if the leaders had not expected it of me. But they did, and I am grateful. I began by observing lessons written by my teacher. She critiqued my work and ran it through a review committee before the lessons went out to the classes.

Also look for women talented in computer graphics and visual arts. Enlist their help in producing an attractive lesson that is functional and beautifully highlights your Bible study theme—online and on paper.

Helpful Resources

For a sample lesson, see Appendix B.

WILL YOU RAISE UP YOUR OWN TEACHERS OR RELY ON VIDEO TEACHERS?

The Unintended Consequences of Video Studies

We believe that one of the most disturbing trends in women's Bible studies today is the large percentage of ministries that now rely completely on video teachers. This practice radically changes the environment, discouraging gifted women from identifying, developing, and using their own spiritual gifts. God has blessed women in every congregation and ministry with teaching gifts to serve and minister to others. Women denied the opportunity to use their spiritual gifts will never grow and mature as God desires. When these women take a risk and step out to do something as challenging as teaching the Bible, they experience the supernatural enabling of the Holy Spirit and their faith balloons. They experience what God can do through them.

Then when women gifted in other ways see women from within their own circles step out and use their upfront gifts, they are encouraged to step out too, even when their role is serving behind the scenes. Your army of volunteers naturally evolves. The whole dynamic of raising up women to minister to one another floods the atmosphere and energizes the level of passion and excitement about what God wants to do through ordinary women. However, if "ordinary" teachers must compete with "professionally orchestrated women on the wall," most will shy away from even trying. Relying on video teachers, no matter their level of expertise or charisma, extinguishes the entire process.

Also, attendees without an awareness of the unintended consequences of a steady diet of video studies often clamor for their particular favorite teacher. Groupies easily emerge, making the study as much about the personality of the video teacher as God's Word. In time you may be faced with the same situation Paul wrote about in his letter to the church in Corinth.

> My brothers and sisters, some from Chloe's household have informed me that there are quarrels among you. What I mean is this: One of you says, "I follow Paul"; another, "I follow Apollos"; another, "I follow Cephas"; still another, "I follow Christ." Is Christ divided? Was Paul crucified for you? Were you baptized into the name of Paul? (1 Cor. 1:11–13)

Healthy ministry doesn't highlight any human personality. To eliminate this danger, I love developing teams of teachers with different personalities. Not only does this relieve the time strain on each individual teacher, but I also find that different women prefer different teachers. The focus turns to the Lord rather than on individuals.

If we hear a male pastor encourage women leaders to use primarily video studies, we feel like asking him, "Why don't you just play Chuck Swindoll videos in your church services? He's likely a better preacher than you are, and you won't have to write or preach any more sermons." He probably won't, because he understands how much that practice would injure his relationships and influence with the people in the congregation. The same principles apply with ministry to women.

Postmoderns Insist

Postmodern women want to know their teachers personally. They want to learn from a woman who can answer their questions, and they want to see her model what she teaches. They want to know she's available with hugs and warm personal words.

George Cladis asserts,

> The postmodern world wants to know the heart of its leadership. Words like *authentic* and *genuine* are being used to describe effective and able leaders. The most important question for those who would follow a leader is no longer, "Does she have the educational and professional requirements to fill this position?" but rather, "Is she trustworthy and will she listen to my concerns?"[31]

Many young women who've grown up in the church expect video teachers because that's all they've ever known. However, the vast number of young unbelievers say video teachers seem fake, inauthentic, and showy, qualities that are a definite turn-off to investigators desiring to learn more about Christianity. Even Christian fence-sitters express their dislike of ministries predominantly taught by video teachers. Listen to the plea of postmodern Sarah Bessey in her blog, "Why We Don't Need Women's Ministry":

> You know what I would have liked . . . I would have liked the women of the church to share their stories or wisdom with one another, no more celebrity speakers, please just hand the microphone to the lady over there that brought the apples.[32]

You may argue that the quality of the study will suffer with teachers raised up from among you. You don't have a woman in your church who will ever teach like the "experts." Maybe not—but you might. These "experts" all started somewhere. Even if you don't have a potential Priscilla Shirer, a living teacher who knows your women intimately will be a better fit in time.

The Powerful Appeal of Video Studies

Studies with supplementary videos appeal so strongly to leaders because the studies do much of the work for you, especially if you may lack time and support, you feel overwhelmed, or you struggle with feelings of inadequacy. Just pop in the video. No worries about identifying gifted women, training them, or relying on them. Easy, yes, but truly transformational?

For all the reasons cited, consider raising up your own teachers. Ask God to enable you to transition to live women teachers in time. If you've been using videos for years, you may need to change gradually. You might shorten the video time or eliminate it altogether occasionally at first, substituting a live teacher. If your novice teacher is just learning, ease her into the role by asking her to speak for a short time, maybe ten minutes, and extend the time from there.

These made-to-order video packages are useful when live teachers need a break or to help you get started—especially if you are resource-poor. We use them in the summer when attendance is sporadic. However, make it your goal to wean yourself from video studies as fast as you can for all the reasons we've cited.

We hope these ideas will jump-start a transformational process in your church. Teaching skills can improve through the years. We all need a place to begin. Provide an opportunity for women to use their gifts and watch God work wonders!

WILL YOU OFFER MANY DIFFERENT STUDIES OR JUST ONE?

Think back to the story of postmodern Ashley at the beginning of this chapter. Remember her experience in a room filled with several hundred Christians worshiping, discussing the Bible, and praying together? She left desiring to know more about Jesus. Experiencing the Christian community together is a powerful evangelistic tool—and it energizes believers too.

Our preference is to offer one study on a book of the Bible that all your women can enjoy. And if you have the facilities, bring them together in a large room for worship, teaching, and prayer. But also be sure to divide them up into small groups for more intimate fellowship.

Consider These Issues

How large is your church? How many women participate in the study? If fewer than fifteen women attend, choose a book of the Bible that best meets the needs of that group, and study that book. But as your study grows, you will need to divide the women into small groups. Small group structures will be discussed in depth in chapter 8.

When deciding whether the groups will study the same material or whether you will offer choices, carefully consider your resources, especially the number of teachers you have and the size of your facility. If you have several teachers who want to develop their gifts, or if your facility won't hold everyone, give your women the choice of different studies.

Create Excitement

Even if you offer multiple studies but want to create excitement and a sense of broader community, think about bringing the women together sometime during the study. This energizes the whole group.

During IBC Bible study sessions, women met in the sanctuary around tables. As our study grew, we moved some groups out of the large room and into smaller spaces, where women who were distracted by the noise level held their discussion. They then returned to the main room for announcements, service opportunities, teaching, and prayer. Learning the Bible and worshiping God together with sisters creates a joyful ethos. During the concert of prayer, I was often near tears listening to the sacred sounds of women praying around their tables in their small groups.

Create Connections

You will discover other advantages to everyone studying the same curriculum. Friends enjoy discussing the concepts they are studying even if they do not meet in the same small group. Our men's evening group met at the same time, often studying the same material. Then couples interacted over the material at home. If you have a children's program, consider having the kids study a scaled-down version of mom's study.

Create Continuity

Design your studies with long-term benefit in mind. For example, the first year I taught at IBC, I taught the Gospel of Luke. I wanted the women to know Jesus. The next year we studied Acts. I entitled the series "Acts of the Spirit" because the study focused on the work of the Holy Spirit in the first-century church and in our lives today.

The third year I taught "Love Letters from Paul: A Study of Five Epistles." This study built on the founding of the churches in Acts. As we dissected the letters Paul wrote to those churches, we learned key doctrines necessary for living the Christian life. Over these three years, the women came to know Jesus, the Holy Spirit, and key Christian doctrines. The fourth year we studied the covenants to give women an understanding of God's panoramic promises from Genesis to Revelation.

We laid a solid foundation for the myriads of new believers coming into our church. But the material also challenged women who had walked with the Lord for many years.

Plan a curriculum that aligns with your purpose, find a format that works for you, and tackle it with passion. Remember: women are transformed through an intimate relationship with Jesus, and you are the matchmaker.

WHAT KINDS OF CURRICULUM KEEP WOMEN IN THE WORD?

A Curriculum That Requires Homework

The most important part of your Bible study occurs *before* the women gather. The best lessons require homework. This format encourages your women to find a quiet place where they can reflect on the passage and commune with God. The lesson you provide is merely the tool God uses to deepen the relationship.

A Curriculum That Offers Choices

A Bible study that transforms lives brings women of different ages and life stages together. Titus 2 mandates that mature women mentor women less advanced in the process. Often the more mature women have studied the Bible longer. How will you keep your women challenged while not overwhelming those new to Bible study? You give the women choices in the same lesson.

I write studies with two levels. Again, see Appendix B for a sample lesson. Here are two levels I usually include in each lesson.

1. Core-Level Questions

I always write a core level for new believers and busy women. I have also learned that some women won't spend as much time on their lesson as others. This doesn't always mean the studious women are more mature. Often it reflects the woman's gifts.

For example, a woman with the gift of pastoring or encouragement tends to focus on relationships. She comes to Bible study to interact with others. Her priority is to hear about their lives, encourage them, and pray for them. However, a woman with the gift of teaching loves to sit for hours at her desk lost in study. She attends Bible study to focus on the lesson. God designed us differently. One way to meet diverse needs is to provide options in the lessons for the great variety of women God entrusts to you.

The core-level questions require one or two hours of study time weekly and provide a basic understanding of the text. The core level consists of at least three kinds of questions:

A. Observation Questions
   These questions force the student to look carefully at what the passage says. Most observation questions can be answered from the text.

B. Interpretation Questions
   These questions ask the student to decide what the passage means—first for the original audience, then for us today. Often these questions cause the student to think critically about the way God works in the world and what he wants for his children.

C. Application Questions

These questions challenge students to examine their own lives in light of the truths they are studying and to adjust their thoughts, actions, and attitudes. Small groups often spend more time on application questions because most women love to share their lives with others and because that's where life change happens. You may want to spend more time on the application questions but don't skip the observation and interpretation questions altogether. Jumping to application too quickly is the pitfall of some Bible studies and small group discussions.

We cover most of the core-level questions in the small group discussion. If a woman is faithful every week in her study of the core questions, she will be amazed how much she will learn over several years. I encourage the new and busy women not to be intimidated by women who have more time to study or who have different gifts.

2. Digging-Deeper Questions

Some women want to learn more about the passage. The digging-deeper questions suggest parallel passages to compare and contrast. They require outside resources such as an atlas, Bible dictionary, or concordance. They challenge the students to learn more about history, culture, and geography.

Due to time restrictions, the digging-deeper questions may not be covered in the discussion groups. Nevertheless, women who want more depth in their study have the option. Because it is critical not to discourage new women, and at the same time to provide challenge for mature women, consider offering choices within the same lesson, allowing women of different maturity levels to interact together, encouraging the Titus 2 benefits.

Once you have chosen your Bible study curriculum, you are ready to shape your study.

A Woman of Influence
JEN WILKIN
by Natalie Edwards

Jen Wilkin's trailblazing Bible studies continue to open doors for women to grow in a love for the Word of God. Teacher, shepherd, and Bible expositor, Jen began teaching seven women in her living room. Her tenure as Women's Ministry Director in Houston for five years coupled with her Flower Mound Women's Bible Study, which she began and taught for five years, propelled her into new opportunities for ministry at The Village Church.

Jen is now the Director of Classes and Curriculum at The Village Church Institute, overseeing adult classes for both men and women. Her favorite aspect of her role is teaching the weekly Women's Bible Class at the Flower Mound campus. Jen's contribution to biblical literacy extends worldwide through books and Bible studies such as *None Like Him*, *Women of The Word,* and *1 Peter: A Living Hope in Christ* Bible Study.

Her passion for teaching women emanates from the connections flourishing in this kind of atmosphere. Jen finds teaching women in a single gender context provides richness to conversation and vulnerability for women to connect with other women. Jen affirms the need for women's ministry in the church saying, "While it may not be tragic not to have an annual brunch, I believe women's Bible study accomplishes an indispensable piece of discipleship. Rather than cutting it, I hope churches will return it to a purer definition of 'Bible study' with leaders who are equipped to teach, lead, and counsel."

Jen hails from Wichita Falls, Texas, and chose to follow the Lord at a young age. Exposed to seven different denominations in her faith upbringing, Jen maintains the conviction that the Word of God is the only reliable, unchanging truth. This fuels her passion for biblical literacy in the church.

When not teaching, Jen enjoys a good book and the art of gardening. Jen resides in Flower Mound, Texas, with her family. She has been married more than twenty-five years to husband, Jeff, whom she met at Texas A&M. Together they have four children: Matt, Mary Kate, Claire, and Calvin.

CHAPTER 7

SHAPE YOUR STUDY

Our goal is to unleash women into the world to change it for Christ. Does Bible study *really* equip them? Consider the ripple effect of Bible study in this true-life example.

Every Monday night, Creusa and Sofia were faithful to attend Bible study. But I wasn't aware of their involvement in a local inner-city ministry until I read the ministry's weekly report sent out by its executive director.

> My heart has been breaking over the Hispanic ministry—we needed someone to replace Reverend Martinez to lead the Spanish Bible study. His duties at church would not allow him to continue. For two weeks, I tried the best I could with my tourist Spanish and a Spanish/English Bible to teach the faithful.
>
> Saturday two new volunteers, Creusa and Sofia, answered the call. Our faithful Hispanic neighbors walked in the rain—some twelve blocks with only a towel to keep dry—to hear the Word. We hugged them and introduced them to Creusa and Sofia.
>
> What a joy to hear Creusa ask me, "We have three who want to pray to receive Jesus. Do you want to join us for prayer?" Tears of intercession turned to tears of joy as Mr. Pedro, an older gentleman, little nine-year-old Erendida, who has a hole in her heart, and her older brother, each prayed to receive Christ.

Two days later I received this e-mail from the director:

> Sue, I am so excited about the way Creusa and Sofia have stepped up to the plate to organize the Hispanic Bible study . . . one plants,

105

another waters, another harvests . . . you have part of that harvest
from what you have planted in their lives in your Bible studies!

We don't know whether the women we teach and train will minister to
other women or to children, youth, family, neighbors, or the world. And
we really don't care. We simply want them to get out there and make a
difference—like Creusa and Sofia! How will we shape a Bible study that
turns out an army of unstoppable women?

KEEP IN MIND YOUR SIZE

The most common characteristic of dynamic women's ministries around
the country is the content of their study—the Bible. Churches of any and
every size can implement these foundational truths in the lives of their
women. The differences lie in the details. How does such a ministry get
started? What does a church need to consider?

The answers to these and other questions we will raise in this chapter
depend upon the size of each church and the number of resources available to it. If you minister in a small church with few resources and a small
group of women, your organizational concerns will be few. Ministry will
be fairly simple.

The larger your church, the more complicated the task of providing
quality, exciting ministry. Conversely, a church with many resources has
the ability to offer multiple ministries and diverse opportunities.

Read this chapter with an eye to your own circumstances. Much of this
may not be necessary (or even possible) for small, newly formed ministries.
Take what you can use and apply it passionately. Larger, more established
ministries can benefit from the topics we cover. We wanted to include every
possibility, so that no matter the size of your ministry, your women will be
involved in a Spirit-led flexible but well-organized, well-planned means to
spiritual growth.

WHO WILL LEAD THE BIBLE STUDY?

Ask God for a woman with the gift of administration, a passion for his
Word, and a love for women. Find a woman with experience in managing
a ministry, a family, an organization, or the secular equivalent. Look for a

woman with an eye for detail, a shepherd's heart, and the willingness to both delegate and lead. The ideal leader possesses flexibility, values differences in women, and can adjust when necessary. If a woman with these gifts or experience is not available, find a woman who is teachable.

Two Gifted, Teachable Women

Linda and Barb served on our team as the morning and evening Bible class coordinators. Neither had ever overseen an organization the size of our studies. One year our night class enrolled about four hundred and our morning class about two hundred. Both Linda and Barb were overwhelmed. After our first team leaders meeting, they expressed concern that they were "square pegs in a round hole."

Linda

Linda was terrified of speaking in front of such a large group. Each week to begin the study she had to lead the group in prayer; later in the morning she would make announcements communicating ministry highlights and opportunities to serve. She was diabetic, and I was concerned that the stress would affect her blood sugar. For the first few weeks I watched her quietly, praying that she would overcome her fear and hoping she wouldn't pass out.

On the last day of class, not only did Linda pray and make the announcements, she also shared a ten-minute testimony! She stood on the stage in front of the microphone and spoke to several hundred women with God's confidence. Her words warmed my heart:

> When Sue first approached me and asked me to take this job, I couldn't believe she was asking *me*—I was honored, yet scared out of my mind. Again my past haunted me, and I had no confidence in myself. Sue stretched me and challenged me beyond what I ever thought I could accomplish. We are very fortunate to have a women's pastor who stands alongside our heavenly Father to enable him to complete the work he has begun in us.
>
> I am thankful that God has allowed me this opportunity to serve him and you. It has been a very rewarding job. Just think, if there had been nobody to refresh my spirit or no one who

expected something great out of me, I would still be sitting outside the Bible study group afraid to speak up for the Lord and wondering what my purpose is here on earth.

When Linda retired from the lead team, she didn't leave women's ministry. She served as a spiritual mother to women with acute needs and taught workshops at our retreats and in seminars. Linda says her life was transformed by the experience. It was just the beginning. Now that she lives in another city, Linda leads the Bible study in her church.

Barb

Mother of six and the wife of a pilot, Barb organized a busy household, raised a family, and supported her husband as the military moved them many times. This, and years in a parachurch Bible study, prepared her for the position of evening Bible study coordinator.

But she did not realize the value of her experience and the way God had gifted her to oversee the class. A few times she expressed concern that this ministry was too much and that she wasn't the right person to oversee it. I knew differently, and I was right.

She recruited her leaders early, delegated well, and planned out each class. The study ran like a royal wedding. Barb's life was transformed, and she continues to be instrumental in transforming others.

Pray diligently for God to show you the woman he wants to oversee the Bible class. Because the Bible study is the place women fall in love with Jesus and connect intimately with him and each other, the leader is crucial. Invest in her and unleash her. Then stand back and watch God work.

WHO WILL TEACH THE BIBLE STUDY?

How do you discover Bible teachers? You provide opportunities for them to teach. You ask women to share a short devotional at lead team meetings or a short testimony at the retreat. You observe the process and watch for a supernatural connection with the students.

A woman with the gift of teaching loves to study. She delights in finding ways to help her students learn. She invests hours and hours reading and chewing on concepts God leads her to teach. But just because she is gifted does not mean she won't be nervous initially. If you encourage her, the fear will ultimately subside for the joy of doing what she loves—teaching.

Sue's Experience

My spiritual mother, Kathy Hyde, was like a bird dog tracking teachers. She planted six Bible classes and needed teachers for her team. She recruited leaders in each class and insisted they attend a leader's meeting each week after the class was dismissed.

For me, the leader's meeting was the highlight of the week. We practiced leading the lesson for the next week. We prayed for our groups and for each other. And every leader was required to give at least one mini-lecture a year. Some leaders were so frightened by this assignment, they threatened to quit—but none ever did.

Kathy assigned a mini-lecture topic and asked each leader to speak for about ten minutes. New leaders had the choice of giving their testimony or speaking on the assigned topic. Often the topics would coordinate with the Bible study for that semester.

For example, if we studied Ephesians, we would choose a related topic such as grace or unity. We taught a Bible verse because she wanted us to teach the Bible rather than present a topical message. She showed us how to create a simple outline that helped us develop our message. She taught us how to find illustrations and stories that brought the message alive. Out of that simple assignment emerged Bible teachers who continue to teach the Scriptures in a variety of churches and Bible classes.

Is Seminary an Option?

If you've identified women with teaching gifts but they lack training, several options exist, including seminary. If a campus is not local, most seminaries today offer degrees that are designed to meet the needs of distance learners. For example, I teach a course entitled "Women Teaching Women" that prepares women to teach the Bible expositionally at several of our campuses in formats that work for women who live all over the country.

If a seminary degree is impossible, different organizations sponsor various helpful courses. With the many resources available today, a woman can train herself. I learned to teach the Bible through a parachurch women's Bible study before I attended seminary, although seminary training upped my effectiveness and helped decrease my prep time immeasurably.

In addition, doors opened that probably would not have opened otherwise. Not everyone can attend seminary, but if you can, go for it!

If seminary isn't possible, read books on teaching. Listen to skilled teachers. Attend workshops and seminars. Pray for God's enabling because teaching is far too overwhelming to do in your own strength. Then teach. It's a skill and, like any skill, requires years to do well.

WHERE WILL YOUR STUDY MEET?

You can meet in a home, church, recreation center, or any other centrally located and comfortable facility. If your ministry consists of one or two small groups, a home atmosphere is intimate. However as you begin to grow you will need more space. In addition, you need to set up childcare facilities as soon as possible for moms.

Most studies end up in a church where there is little expense, if any. Churches also typically include childcare facilities. As you add small groups that unite for a portion of the study, you will need a large room where you can spread out your tables.

Circles—Not Rows

Why round tables? Because they facilitate interaction. They give women a place to put their Bibles, their coffee, and their muffins. They increase a sense of unity as we gather in a circle to share what God is doing in our lives. As women meet face-to-face around a circle, they connect.

Classroom-style seating in rows communicates that the emphasis is on the woman up front. In the Transformation Model we don't want to spotlight the leaders. We want to spotlight relationships—first with Jesus and then with others, focusing on what's going on internally in the women's hearts and minds.

Provide Comfort

Whether your groups meet in a large room together, in small rooms individually, or in some combination, ensure adequate lighting and a comfortable temperature. Consider the needs of the elderly and those with chronic pain when you choose rooms and seating.

Welcome Newcomers

Create a user-friendly online registration form with payment options included. Keep paper versions available both at church and at the beginning of each study. Visitors should be able to register themselves and their children, obtain study guides, and find their table. Friendly greeters and a well-organized process make a big impression every week.

The class coordinator provides a master list that shows which groups have openings. If the newcomer arrives with a friend or requests a particular group, try to accommodate her. After a woman registers, one of the greeters walks her to her table and introduces her to the leader. First impressions are important!

WHEN WILL YOU MEET?

Who are your women? All moms work, but do some work for a paycheck? Do single women attend your church? Do you have stay-at-home moms who would prefer to gather during the day? Consider all the women's needs as you plan when to meet. Women's ministry should be inclusive—postmoderns and moderns. I told our women that there were two prerequisites for involvement: you must be a woman and you must show up. Pick a time in which everyone can participate.

If you have the resources, consider two classes—one in the evening and one in the morning. Our evening and daytime classes are identical except the evening class is fifteen minutes shorter to accommodate children's bedtimes.

Does your church serve an evening meal during the week to complement a variety of activities? You might consider piggybacking on what's already in place. Otherwise find a time that does not conflict with other activities and block out that time on the church calendar for a year. Soon everyone will know that this is Bible study time and they will plan their activities around yours.

HOW LONG WILL YOU MEET?

Women's time is precious, so make every minute meaningful. You must allow enough time to incorporate all the elements of a transforming experience without wasting time. Consider how the length of your study affects the women and their families or work. For example, how soon can your

women get there from work? When do children need to be in bed? Will
mothers need to leave to pick up kindergarteners?

Consider the pace of your community. We met for two hours. Women
in morning classes may want to linger while those in evening classes need
to get home and prepare for the next day. Think through what will work
in your particular setting.

Listen to women of all ages and stages and make decisions accordingly.
Be willing to adjust your start time if you notice that a majority of your
women are arriving late or leaving early.

WHAT FORMAT WILL YOU CHOOSE?

The old, trite saying "There's more than one way to skin a cat" is perhaps
offensive to cat lovers, but true enough. There are many ways to accomplish
your objectives. And there are many Bible study formats that transform
women. However, all formats should include these elements:

- Bible study
- Community
- Prayer
- Opportunities to use what you learn

You Can't Please Everyone

How you weave the basic elements into a meaningful whole is your choice.
Whatever you choose, you won't make everyone happy. Task-oriented,
bottom-line women attending purely for Bible study would prefer less time
on relationship-building activities, prayer, and sharing. Often women attending primarily for community get restless discussing details of the Bible
lesson and theology. Neither is wrong. Each must guard against extremes
and both can benefit from the others' perspectives.

What if we put all the task-oriented women in one group and those
there for community in another? What if we adjusted the format to make
each group happy? They would like it—but it would not be good for them.

If they are married, their spouses are probably more like the other group.
If they have children or work, they live and work with people in the other
group every day. We all need to appreciate and enjoy the differences.

Those of us who are task-oriented need to loosen up and value relationships. Those who are more interested in community need to redeem time and accomplish something! It's healthy for us to study the Bible together and learn from one another.

Although I love women, I am task-oriented. When I began serving women more than thirty-five years ago, I didn't understand women who were more interested in community. I thought everyone should be like me. As a result, my studies were highly structured with little time for sharing, prayer, or fellowship. I was there to teach the Bible, and they needed to learn it!

But God has opened my eyes to the importance of relationships more and more through the years, and postmoderns demand it. I surround myself with women who keep me balanced and sensitive to the value of different approaches and perspectives. Know yourself and guard against the mistakes I made.

As you decide on a format, be open to change. Do year-end evaluations and tweak your format in response. But don't overreact to each comment. You will never please everyone. As a leader you aren't there to be popular. You are there to transform women. By God's grace, you will earn their respect. So do what you can to give each group what they need, and help each group understand why they need balance.

SAMPLE FORMATS

Your format is like a fine quilt, a variety of pieces precisely stitched together. The end result will create something splendid. Let's look at ways leaders all over the nation structure their studies. Examine these models and extract elements that will work for you.

Altogether Separate

In this format women meet together for parts of the study and meet separately in small groups for others. The choice is yours. Usually you include the same elements in the format each week. You achieve variety by changing the order of the elements or by adding special emphasis days when you offer workshops or something totally different. Consider these options within this format:

All Altogether

Everyone studies the same curriculum and the women do not travel during the study. They meet around tables in small groups in a large room. The room must allow the tables to be spread apart far enough that women can hear as they meet separately in their small groups. With each format you will find advantages and disadvantages.

Advantages:
- They generate excitement by being together.
- Time isn't wasted moving from place to place.
- Worship fills the room as a powerful witness to nonbelievers, energizing everyone.
- You can incorporate arts elements like videos into the teaching.

Disadvantages:
- Some women find it hard to hear during times focused around the table.
- Women at tables located far from the front may feel disconnected from the action during together times. If many of your women are elderly, this format may not work. However, one way to solve the problem is to adopt the next option.

Altogether Some

Some of the groups can remain in the large room while others travel to self-contained spaces for table time. Then these groups can join the large group either at tables or in chairs in rows around the large room. Or all the small groups can meet in separate rooms and come together for teaching, worship, and other communal elements of the format.

Hardly Together

If you offer multiple studies, those studying the same curriculum will need to meet together for small groups, prayer, and teaching. But you can still join together for worship, announcements, and service opportunities.

Half In/Half Out

You don't have to use the same format each week. If your women like change, another way to add variety is to change your format from semester to semester or even week to week.

The downside of using different formats is that they are confusing to administer and confusing to women who don't attend regularly. As long as you keep your format simple, most class coordinators can keep the agenda straight. But if you begin to add multiple elements on top of an inconsistent format, it can be overwhelming.

If a woman misses a few weeks, she may be confused about what to expect the day she returns. Calendars and clear communication help. Some women love chaos while others enjoy routine. Keep both in mind as you plan your format.

Shape your study with prayer considering the needs of the women God sends you. Remember, its form and features will either attract or repel women who want to know God and his Word. You will never design the perfect structure for everyone—it doesn't exist! But you can organize a study that woos women to God's Word, and if they persevere, their lives will be transformed.

A Woman of Influence
REBECCA CARRELL
by Lindsay Ann Nickens

Rebecca Carrell always wanted to do radio. As a little girl, Rebecca was given a tape recorder and she quickly began to record her own radio shows, complete with artist introductions and commercial breaks. Having grown up on stage and enjoying the interaction that entertainment provided, becoming a radio show host was a natural transition for Rebecca.

She began working for a country music radio station in 1998. She was successful in this venture and spent thirteen years as a radio host for the station—a training ground for what was to come. Behind the microphone, however, was a broken young woman, suffering from alcoholism and bulimia. Rebecca had begun experimenting with bulimia at thirteen, and it quickly turned into a twenty-year battle.

In 2009 everything changed. In what Rebecca calls a "miraculous delivery," God broke the chains of alcoholism in an instant and began to renew her mind, moving her away from bulimia and towards a greater understanding of his love for her. Knowing that God was shifting the ground beneath her towards ministry, Rebecca left country radio in 2011 and began volunteering at a mom's ministry at her church, writing curriculum and leading twelve women in Bible studies.

Once healed from her struggle with bulimia, Rebecca immediately began to receive invitations to tell her testimony, speak at churches, and lead retreats. An employee of KCBI radio who had heard Rebecca's testimony contacted her and asked her to fill in as a host for KCBI's morning show for eight weeks. She struggled, fasting and praying regularly; how could she go back to radio when God was so clearly calling her to ministry? She felt, though, that God was leading her in this direction, and so she began the temporary position.

During her time in this position, Rebecca heard something curious: the employees of KCBI did not call themselves a "radio station" but a "ministry." Suddenly it dawned on her that this was a God-designed marriage of the two things about which she was most passionate, radio and ministry.

With a new general manager came a new opportunity to remain as a morning show host. Rebecca took the job gladly, and continues to serve in this capacity. On top of her radio position, Rebecca keeps a full speaking schedule and is trailblazing the way for KCBI's ministry to women. She hosts a yearly conference, Heartstrong Faith, devoted to enriching women's understanding of the Bible in order to grow their faith in Christ.

Rebecca currently studies at Dallas Theological Seminary, pursuing her ThM, while also being a wife to Michael Carrell and mom to Caitlyn and Nicholas. Her education at DTS has caused her to become even more enthusiastic about opportunities to encourage women to grow deeper in their understanding of Scripture.

CHAPTER 8

FEATURE SMALL GROUPS

"Mack says me and the kids have to move out by May 1. He owns the house and we have to leave. Do I need a lawyer? How will I pay one?" asked Jessie. Her eyes were swollen and she spoke in monotone. She described their four-year marriage, a second marriage for both. Her three children, now nine, eleven, and sixteen, had never bonded with Mack, and Mack had not spoken to them in over a month.

He had never hit her, although a year earlier he had thrown her against a wall, frightening her so much she called 911. But Mack told the police she was lying, and because there were no physical signs of abuse, the police simply filed a report, warning them that if there were a second offense, someone would go to jail. Since then he no longer raged. Now he was silent and mean.

Mack began attending another church, where he joined a divorce recovery class—even though he wasn't divorced. When Jessie found out, she showed up at the class and embarrassed him. Her response added to his anger.

Jessie did not move out May 1, but she did retain a lawyer to look after their interests. Over the next two years, I (Sue) worked with Jessie as she transitioned from a wife to a single parent. Mack refused to make any effort to heal their marriage, but Jessie continued to hope—until one August night.

Mack continued to demand they leave—with greater and greater insistence. We later learned that he was pursuing another woman who didn't know he was married. On August 14, Jessie dropped the kids off at church for AWANA, shopped for groceries, and drove home. As she approached the driveway, she saw her daughter's puppy dead in the street.

Nine-year-old Mandy named him Fudsie because his chocolate brown coat was sprinkled with tan, which Mandy said were the nuts. Now his coat was stained red, but not from an automobile. His little neck was twisted and blood spotted his face and neck. Jessie was grateful Mandy was not with her. She ran into the house.

"What happened to Fudsie?" she demanded.

"Oh, he got out," answered Mack, but his sneer was evident. She knew he would never admit the truth. She walked into the bedroom to try to clear her head. Mack followed her. Suddenly he was in her face. He began to rage and rail with obscenities. He knew her vulnerabilities and used them as he followed her from room to room. Jessie began to cry. Then she felt a hot anger burning from within and she gave into it. When he grabbed her arm, she slapped him. He smiled.

This time Mack called 911. When the police arrived, Jessie was still angry. She tried to explain what he had done to her daughter's puppy. But Mack had a different story and they believed him.

As a friend rounded the corner bringing the children home, they saw their mom being handcuffed and put into a police car. Fudsie still lay dead in the street.

Hope was gone. Jessie was released, but the judge required that she attend an anger management class and was put on probation for a year. She moved out immediately and began a journey to rebuild her life and help her children rebound. Mack's girlfriend wised up, and he tried to see Jessie several times over the next year.

She agonized over whether or not his advances were genuine. They went to a professional counselor, but in the end Mack resisted the work assigned and filed for divorce.

This is real women's ministry. It's messy and often heartbreaking. True, this example sounds extreme, but it is not uncommon. What can we do as leaders to help women like Jessie?

First, consider if the situation calls for legal intervention. Familiarize yourself with current statutes regarding domestic violence and abuse.

Even if the situation is not that extreme, we need more than programs and parties. We must create an ethos where women feel safe seeking help from the church. Small groups can provide systematic support from God's Word and God's people. Only through intimacy with Christ and authentic community can a woman like Jessie find the inner strength to rebuild her life.

I met with Jessie periodically, but my ministry partner was her small group leader. She had the experience and the heart to help Jessie. In addition to weekly calls, her leader planned a weekend retreat at a lake house for her small group. They ate popcorn in their pajamas, talking late into the night. Jessie's small group was the community God used to keep her close to him, to enable her to overcome her circumstances, and to teach her how to respond to them biblically.

WHY SMALL GROUPS?

So far we have discussed how to organize the overall study. Did you notice that we assume you will incorporate small groups into your ministry? Small groups are not an option. Why?

In part 1 we saw that postmodern women are starving for relationships. This was evident from the panel Sue attended at Multnomah, where the young women kept wishing for a "home." Their voices trembled as they pleaded with women leaders to remember their need to connect. Small groups serve as "home" in your study.

Most modern women love fellowship too. God created women to be relational as a reflection of his triune character. Women should never be ashamed of enjoying relationships. Building relationships—first with Jesus and then with each other—is the second pillar of the Transformation Model, second only to centering on Scripture. Small groups are the means to relationship and thus transformation.

Therefore we encourage you to invest prayer, time, and resources into building your small groups. It is a key priority. Let's analyze the small group process.

WHAT'S THE IDEAL MAKEUP OF A SMALL GROUP?

The best small groups are mixed in age, spiritual maturity, and life-stage experiences. As evidenced in the biblical mandate in Titus 2, God desires that we put women of different ages together. In my experience, if we teach the younger women to take the initiative, natural Titus 2 mentoring friendships emerge out of the mixed small group. In addition, it is healthy for women to come in contact with all kinds of women. However, that does not mean we draw their names out of a hat when we divide up the groups.

Organic Approaches to Finding Community

Some postmoderns balk at being placed in a group of women they don't know. They feel uncomfortable joining a group of strangers with the goal of building intimate relationships and studying the Bible together.

One church sponsors four gatherings to give women an opportunity to connect informally before they place them in small groups. Leaders facilitate teaching and discussion during the first half of each session. Participants talk through questions with those in their cluster for the remaining half. Participants are given freedom where to sit and begin to cultivate connections with those they meet. After six weeks, each person writes down the names of those they desire to be in a group with. Then groups are formed based on these connections in tandem with day/time meeting preferences. This approach fosters choice and authentic connection with hopes of building sustainable groups.

Other churches allow small groups to stay together indefinitely to overcome this resistance to "forced community." Do all you can to help women overcome opposition, but ultimately ministries cannot function without organization and order. However, guard against unnecessary structure and rigidity.

The complex reasons that fuel this opposition are beyond the scope of this book. For insight, read *Organic Mentoring*, which I (Sue) wrote with Barbara Neumann. In her doctoral research, Barbara interviewed young women to understand more about the differences between postmodern and modern women. Her conclusions were invaluable.

How to Construct a Small Group

The process of group selection is prayer-based, time-consuming, and critical to women's transformation. Here are some guidelines:

Recruit a Team

If possible, provide every group with two leaders—a discussion leader and a coleader. You can call these leaders shepherds, spiritual mothers, or anything else you want.

Limit the Size

The optimum size of a small group is a weekly attendance of eight to ten. That's how many you want participating each week, so consider making the official group size larger, because after the first couple of weeks, a few women will miss every week because of illness, travel, or family responsibilities. A more intimate group of five or six works well if the women show a high commitment level. But in most studies, you attract both responsible women, those who give up easily, and women overwhelmed with life.

Make the group large enough to create interesting discussions but small enough for intimate sharing, individual participation, and effective facilitation by the small group leader. Expect that your attendance will fluctuate during the semester so that some weeks you may have more than seven and others considerably less. Our goal is for each group to connect, minister to one another, and experience true community.

Pray, Pray, Pray

Build each group carefully and prayerfully. Preregister as many women as possible so you will have an estimate of how many to expect.

Shortly before the semester started, we gathered a small team consisting of the administrator, women's pastor and/or director, and anyone else who knew the women well. We committed our task to God in prayer as we began.

Match Up the Leader and Coleader First

We began by matching up the leadership teams. Identify their giftedness and pair women who complement one another. Categorize these leadership teams according to the women to whom they will most likely connect. Pair empty nesters with new or single moms, working women with others who share their experience.

Place Women in Groups

Either implement the organic method described earlier, in which members took the first few weeks to discover natural affiliations with others, or consider a more traditional approach. The registration forms told us the woman's age, church, marital status, address, if she works, children's ages, if she requests to be with a friend or in a particular group, and other pertinent information.

Then, using the information provided and our personal knowledge of the women, we assigned participants to groups. Remember: mix older women with younger, talkers with quiet ones, and think critically about the leaders to whom you assign nonbelievers, women from different churches/denominations, and women with special circumstances. And be sure to assign strong-willed, opinionated women to experienced leaders.

Finally, we assigned new women where we believed they would thrive.

Take a Final Look

After placing each woman, evaluate the particular makeup of each group. Try to visualize this group interacting. Did you create a good mix? Does the group fit with its leaders? Are there too many talkers? needs? potential problems?

Ask God to show you if your choices reflected his choices. Building groups is a bit like building families. We want them to love and respect each other. We want them to learn from one another. We want meaningful friendships formed that will last a lifetime.

Think of how complex a family of four can be. We are building families of ten! We build with finite understanding, including women we have never even met. It's a wonder any of them work! But they do. Not all, but many. And when they do, we celebrate. When they don't, we know we did the best we could.

Try to leave several openings in each group for women who have not registered and for neighbors who decide at the last minute they will come with friends. If you don't have enough openings, know you will need to recruit new leaders. Entrust the groups to God and work hard to find a good mix. God uses your efforts to transform lives. It is worth every minute.

HOW DO YOU CHOOSE SMALL GROUP LEADERS?

Look for spiritually mature women who love God, his Word, and other women. Look for passionate women who have worked through their emotional baggage and are able to invest in others. Find women who will persevere through challenges and are eager to make a difference. In addition, you want teachable and humble women. You want them willing to work within your parameters and on board with your vision. You probably won't find women that meet all these criteria, but at least find women who desire to become this way.

Generally, draw from women you have observed in the study. Occasionally a woman will join who has extensive experience in another ministry. Recruit her only after careful analysis. Try to find someone who has worked with her. It only takes one difficult leader to make your life miserable and do harm to the study.

Recruit leaders using an adapted version of the process for recruiting a lead team member (in chapter 4). Consider recruiting one or two more than you think you will need in case your numbers swell. Ask them to be on call if they are needed.

WHAT ARE THE DIFFERENT ROLES OF THE LEADER AND COLEADER?

Generally the leader directs the discussion. She is in charge. The coleader assists her and oversees the group's administrative details. See Appendix C for the small group leaders' manual. You will find the roles clearly defined there. Adapt the manual to your study if you find it useful.

You can change the job descriptions of the leader and coleader to fit your purposes. However, we suggest that they do not share leading the discussion. A group grows when it is used to a particular leader's style and finds a change every week confusing.

Some women's temperaments and gifts make them better leaders and others better coleaders. Don't insist that everyone make it her goal to be the leader. Just as everyone in the church is equally valuable to God, let your coleaders know that they are equally valuable to you.

HOW WILL YOU EQUIP YOUR LEADERS AND COLEADERS?

Prioritize your small group leaders training. Without it, your groups will never really thrive. Gather them together periodically for in-depth times of training and interaction. Design a training manual so that they understand what you expect. Again, refer to the sample manual in Appendix C. Give each leader a copy and find creative ways to teach them how to use it. Help them understand that leading small groups is a skill and will take time to master.

Our leaders met for training at least a week before the class kickoff. Set aside at least four hours. Here is a typical agenda for a morning training:

9:00 A.M.   Icebreaker games and goodies as women arrive
- Seat leaders and coleaders together.

9:20 A.M.   Introduce each leader briefly.

9:30 A.M.   Hand out manuals and teach small group leading techniques and strategies.
- Use drama, games, role-play, and other creative teaching tools.
- Let experienced leaders help as the group interacts.
- Break midway, and again at the end.

11:00 A.M.   Class administrator explains how the class operates. and hands out her expectations in writing.
- Hand out group rosters if they are ready.
- Explain and sign conflict resolution covenants, Q and A.

11:20 A.M.   Break for quick box lunch and fellowship

11:45 A.M.   Gather in a circle for mock lesson led by instructor.
- The leaders bring a completed lesson 1 to go over as a model.

12:30 P.M.   Prayer (as a group or as leader teams) for groups, kickoff, teacher, etc.

1:15 P.M.   Dismiss, extend nursery so leader teams can meet until 1:30.
- Trainer stays around to answer questions.

Build on this initial training all year. If you meet periodically as leaders, take ten minutes and review a leading principle. Create a humorous pop quiz to see what your leaders remember. Ask your leaders to share actual situations they have encountered. Enlist everyone's input on how to handle the issue. However, protect confidentiality by asking leaders not to mention names.

Once you learn the skill of leading a small group, you will find many other opportunities to use it. I (Sue) was active in my children's high school, both as band club and PTA president. Once after a meeting a woman who chaired a local political party complimented me: "That's the best-run meeting I ever sat through." I smiled. I was just using the skills I learned leading small groups for Bible study.

We have examined many decisions you need to consider as you plan your Bible study. Use the ideas that work for you. If you are overseeing ministry to women in a small church, the process is simpler. Enjoy a less complex ministry, but understand that God may expand your influence. When women's lives are transformed, often others will follow.

However, growth depends on a variety of factors—the overall growth and health of your church, the support you receive from your leadership, and the experience of your team. We will address these issues in later chapters. For now, work hard and depend completely on the Lord. He is responsible for the results.

A Woman of Influence
PRISCILLA SHIRER
by Natalie Edwards

Founder of Going Beyond Ministries and worldwide notable speaker, Priscilla Shirer preaches God's Word with boldness and power. With a Master of Arts in Biblical Studies from Dallas Theological Seminary, Priscilla's conviction for sound biblical exposition coupled with practical application of the Scriptures resonates with the hearts of women and men worldwide.

Priscilla's unique background of television and radio opened the door for her beginning in speaking. As a radio intern in 1993, Priscilla envisioned a future in television as a news anchor. Yet soon she began receiving invites to speak as listeners encouraged her to start teaching Bible studies in the Houston area. Before long, Priscilla was balancing speaking engagements, Bible studies, and a new mentorship with motivational speaker Zig Ziglar.

Now as a traveling speaker and Bible teacher, Priscilla speaks at conferences such as Passion, Gateway Pink Impact, and Hillsong's Colour Conference. She empowers women through books such as *God Is Able* and Bible studies such as *Discerning the Voice of God* and *The Resolution for Women.* In addition, her ministry Going Beyond gathers women around the country for revival through local outreach events called Awaken. Her podcasts, devotionals, and blogs provide additional resources for women through Going Beyond's website.

In tandem with Priscilla's flourishing ministry in speaking and writing, her character in the movie *War Room* captivated hearts of filmgoers across America. It's a role Priscilla was born to play. For one who imagined a future in television, God opened the perfect door for Priscilla's gift. Her lead actress role as Elizabeth Jordan softened the hearts of those longing to connect deeper with God and reminded us of the power of prayer. Her book *Fervent: A Woman's Battle Plan to Serious, Specific and Strategic Prayer* subsequently followed. Priscilla's crossover role in film and faith continues to open doors in ministering to culture.

Priscilla resides in Dallas, Texas, with her husband of eighteen years, Jerry Shirer, and three sons, Jackson, Jerry Jr., and Jude. As a self-professed "boy mom," Priscilla delights in moments watching her sons participate in sports and play with their golden doodle. Priscilla is the daughter of Tony Evans, pastor of Oak Cliff Bible Fellowship in Dallas, Texas.

CHAPTER 9

ROMANCE THE POSTMODERN WOMAN

ROMANCE HER WITH THE BIBLE AND COMMUNITY

The postmodern woman longs to be loved and romanced. When faith knocks on the door of a woman's heart, it's love that compels her to accept the invitation. This is where you come in. As a woman who seeks to draw other women into the fold, remember your appeal to her heart. Recall God's divine wooing of your soul as the same basis for your own wooing of her soul to God.

Romance her with the truth of the Scriptures, so that her eyes open wide to the revelation that she is a treasure to God. How do you romance a woman with the Scriptures? By letting your own love for the Word of God stir her heart to want it too. Invite her to Bible studies where she can see other women living out their faith in their lifestyle. Let your own closeness with the Lord show her that God is worth pursuing. This will make room for God to woo her.

You'll find that women long for deepness in their spiritual life. Yet many don't know how to find it or how to cultivate it. This is why your authenticity as a follower of God is so important. The postmodern woman wants to know that your faith is real. When she sees that, that's when her heart will be softened. Your passion will stir her passion. Your love for the Word of God will provoke her love for the Word of God. Thus, real, influential community in the life of a woman remains crucial in her spiritual development. The postmodern woman will be moved and challenged to dive into the beauty of God's Word when she sees real life change taking place in her friends.

—Natalie Edwards
(young twenty-something)

Sarah was a twenty-six-year-old newlywed. Five months earlier she and Bryan made a covenant to love and honor each other until death separated them—and they promised to include God in their marriage. But Bryan lost his job right after they returned from their honeymoon. And sex had been extremely painful for Sarah—so much that they still had not had intercourse. Their dream honeymoon bombed and they were both discouraged and disappointed.

Losing his job and feeling rejected, Bryan stopped talking. Finally when he did communicate, he yelled at Sarah, "Any God that would let this happen is a God I don't want to know." He refused to attend church and dropped out of men's Bible study. Bryan's anger only made Sarah more distant physically.

Their marriage spiraled down toward destruction and if they didn't turn it around, they would soon be another statistic. As a women's minister, what can you offer Sarah? Biblical counseling, of course. But more than that.

MINISTERING TO POSTMODERN SARAH

Sarah will need a woman who has walked through her circumstances and come out on the other side intact. She will need God's Word to help her view her marriage from God's perspective. She will need women friends so that she will not expect Bryan to meet all her relational needs. She will need prayer from sisters who want her marriage to succeed and are willing to invest in her life to make that a reality. She will need God and an army of his women.

Rebecca Carrell (see p. 117 for profile) counsels her radio audience regularly: "You can't follow a God you don't trust, and you can't trust a God you don't know. But you can't know God apart from his Word." The postmodern woman craves community where she feels safe, accepted, and loved. Your ministry to women needs to foster this sort of community—a place that allures her to belong because the women there model what they learn. Young women experience a place where the Word of God is so deeply ingrained that the aroma of God's presence floats through the atmosphere. A place where they observe that the Bible is integral to their lives, not merely something to be studied.

Consider changing the name of the group. If calling the group a "community" or "life group" helps, go for it.

Create an ethos designed to transform how women live, think, love, and serve. But it has to be a Bible study where Sarah, as a postmodern woman, feels accepted. It has to be a place where leaders understand postmoderns and are willing to employ methods that work for them.

If we count the hours Sarah will spend at home on her lesson and attending the study, she will invest three to five hours each week. How can we design these hours for maximum impact in Sarah's life—as well as the lives of the modern women needed to mentor her?

MAKE IT AN EXPERIENCE

For all women—but especially for postmodern women—Bible study must be more than an intellectual exercise. It must include a spiritual awakening, an experience that will draw them into an authentic, intimate relationship with God and others. As women go deep into God's Word, witness the powerful impact of faith in others' lives, and take in images of eternal truths through a variety of media, the experience colors the rest of their week. In time, as they cooperate with God, they are transformed.

We saw in chapter 1, *Who Is the Postmodern Woman?*, that many young women demand more than propositional truth. They want to see Jesus lived out in his followers. They want to know if the experience is real.

Please don't misunderstand. We are not advocating that you put out boxes of tissues every week. Our goal is *not* hysteria so women will make decisions based solely on emotion. Don't stop teaching the truths of Scripture through sound, solid reasoning. Just add elements that will move these truths from head to heart.

Why? Because our relationship with Christ involves more than our minds. Yes, it begins there. And we want lessons and teaching that take us deep into the complexities of life and theology. But these truths must transform both our relationships and the way we live. We want women to *love* Jesus, to *love* his Word, and to *love* others. His love has the power to make us overcomers. His love fills the holes in our hearts, and we are made new. Women yearn to be loved. How do we connect them with the love that Jesus yearns to lavish upon them so they can bless others?

LIVE OUT HIS LOVE

We feel loved when others care for us and respect us. We feel loved when others make it clear that they will not withdraw their affection if we let them down. We feel loved when they have our best interests at heart. We feel loved when others care enough to tell us the truth gently.

We show these women love by the way we treat them from the moment they walk in the door. Leaders express love when they create an atmosphere of unconditional acceptance in the groups. We love them when we give them our best.

We all feel loved when caring is expressed in tender ways—through music, praise, special words, and images that travel through our senses and connect us to our loved one. God created us this way. Make it your goal to express the love of Jesus to women during the study. How? What are some practical ways to create experience in your study? Here are some ideas that worked for us.

ADD ART

The Bible is full of powerful stories, songs, poetry, symbols, and images that shout his love for us. Why not incorporate them into the experience? Add art to your format. It is a powerful communicator. Art romances the soul and softens the heart to truth, often revealing God in unique ways.

For centuries art revolved around Christian themes. Visit the great museums and cathedrals around the world and you will see the Bible illustrated in moving masterpieces. Does music influence our world? Every teenager's ear is wired with ear buds. Do images, more than words, impact our thinking? Consider the effect of advertising, social media, and film. Their influence comes from the heart behind the art. As the great Creator, God gave us creativity. Embrace communication tools for God's glory.

I incorporated art in my teaching when I taught in a traditional church. I had few resources. Nevertheless, I handed out outlines decorated with clip art, used visual aids, and displayed paintings on easels if they expressed the theme of my message. I dressed in a band uniform, wore silly hats, and delivered the message in a British accent to make my point. When God called me to a church that used art, I was delirious with the new resources. Use what you have.

I love art, but not all teachers do. If not, God has women in your ministry with artistic abilities who would love to use them to honor him. Look for scriptwriters, actors, singers, musicians, dancers, graphic designers, and technicians. Find women who love the arts and recruit them to help you.

God gifted many women with angelic voices. Others play instruments. Others dance or paint. Locate them and give them opportunities to use their talents to complement the Scriptures. These media can drive the Bible message deep into the hearts of women. It's well known that the more sensory gates through which you can bring information, the better they will retain it.

CENTER THE EXPERIENCE ON A THEME

A Bible passage may contain several themes, so determine which one to emphasize. Who will design the Bible study experience around the theme? Enlist an arts integration team, including the teacher and other creative women in your church.

Plan ahead, because creating effective art elements takes time. Unleash creative women and stand back for an idea explosion.

Here are some ideas to prime the pump:

- What worship songs complement the theme?
- Find a related painting or picture to display on the screens or an easel during the study.
- Find or create a short drama to illustrate the theme. If not, many quality dramas are available both in Christian bookstores and online.
- Can you find a film clip to illustrate the theme or a point in the message? You can buy a license covering many major producers from Christian Video Licensing International. See www.cvli.org. For permission to use videos and films in their entirety or clips not covered by the CVLI license, contact the production companies directly. CVLI will give you the contact information if needed.
- What about a special song that illustrates the theme? Should a group sing it or would it be more effective as a solo or maybe an ensemble of instruments?

- Would a woman signing the words add meaning? We had a woman who signs for the deaf. She blessed us with gracious sweeping movements that powerfully took us into the meaning of the music.
- Maybe a game to play, a question to answer, or a case study to ponder would complement the theme.
- Would a ceremony be meaningful? Could you serve communion, light candles, or nail prayer requests to a cross?
- Explore the use of sound effects to enhance the experience. During a lesson on the rainbow covenant, we played the sound of rain in the background.
- Would a special food complement the theme? During the lesson on the Holy Spirit, the teacher treated us to *Dove* chocolate bars.
- Which visual aids might enhance the experience? During the lesson on the armor of God, we spotlighted a life-size suit of armor standing on a draped platform. To enhance a theme on our value to God, we gave out pretend million-dollar bills.
- Can a woman share a related story or testimony?
- Do you have special books on the theme you want to give away? We gave away a related book weekly at the beginning to encourage punctuality.
- Make a bookmark using a poem, story, or piece of art for the women to take home. What other mementos could your team create?
- What costume could the teacher wear to illustrate her message?
- Should we all wear something related to the message? We wore party hats to celebrate God's work in our lives and jogging suits when the theme was spiritual health.
- Perform a magic trick to illustrate the theme. Once I used chemicals to illustrate forgiveness. I poured black water into a glass pitcher. Then I added a red solution and the water instantly turned clear.
- Could a dance be choreographed to illustrate your message?

Remember: honor all copyrights and obtain permission if necessary.

What other ideas come to mind? Use them as tools to enhance the experience. However, be careful not to use too many at one time. Too much can overwhelm the senses. Our worship always complemented the theme. We normally displayed some kind of art that announced the theme as soon as the women walk in. Choose the strongest elements for that theme and do them with excellence. Yes, it's work, but the results are worth it.

TEACH MESSAGES THAT EMPHASIZE APPLICATION

In seminary we learned to think theologically. We studied every book of the Bible as well as a variety of views on almost every theological subject. We learned to think propositionally, to reason carefully, and to apply biblical truth to everyday life. Our training was invaluable and provided resources for teaching that help us constantly.

Most women (and for that matter most seminarians) don't care about the difference between supra- and superlapsarianism. That is especially true of postmodern women. Today mothers and grandmothers come to church asking, "Who is preaching and what's their subject?" But postmoderns ask, "Who will be there, and will they accept me?" They want to know if they can find a *home* and they want to see if God and our faith are real.

Therefore, our big idea needs to be practical. Our message outline points need to relate to real life with words like *you* and *us*. And our message should be full of illustrations and stories that bring theoretical truths alive. This has always been good teaching. But it is even more critical today because postmodern women aren't impressed merely with our scholarship. They want to see if our faith works.

TEACH WOMEN TO CONNECT

That may sound ridiculous. Don't women know how to connect? Yes and no. Most women are eager for friendships, but many live in isolation because they are bound by fear. They have never lived in a functioning family. People, especially their parents, let them down. They are desperate to connect but suspicious that you will wound them.

Americans are taught to be independent. We live next door and across the street—yet we remain strangers. Our calendars are so full of activity that there's little time for relationships. We work long hours, play hard, and are entertainment junkies. Technology both connects and divides us. Friendships are often not a priority.

Teachers can help women connect. One year at IBC I taught Titus so I could hammer home God's mandate to older and younger women. I shared the way my spiritual mother nurtured me and I challenged them to nurture each other.

I instructed the younger women to take the initiative if they wanted to be mentored by an older woman. I helped them understand that an older woman was not going to approach them with words like, "I've learned some things I think would help you, dear. Would you like to get together?"

We want mentoring relationships to occur naturally as a byproduct of women spending time together in Bible study. And they do. But often women need encouragement and training. We offered a class on spiritual mothering in the summer and over fifty women signed up. Women want to minister to one another. Teach them.

PROVIDE TIME FOR WOMEN TO CONNECT

What good is teaching women to connect if we never give them time? I would love to have had an hour each week to teach. But I usually got only twenty-five to thirty minutes. I learned that time spent interacting was just as important as time spent listening to me. For some, it was more important.

Our first session of the year, we set aside a block of time for women to get acquainted. Monthly we extend our time of fellowship around a meal. We encourage our leaders to take their groups on an overnight retreat during the first semester. Leaders plan several gatherings outside of class.

Leaders and coleaders split the roster and connect with the women regularly. They send text messages and write notes. They schedule coffees together. They sing to women on their birthdays. They bring flowers, candles, and snacks to brighten up their tables. I am often overwhelmed by the creative ways they express love to the women in their groups. It's all part of the experience!

TEACH WOMEN TO PRAY AND GIVE THEM TIME TO PRAY

We wait for several weeks before we pray together in the groups. Why? Because many are terrified to pray out loud! A few quit the class when they learn we pray together.

Carol came to us three years ago from another church. In her tradition, they did not study the Bible and they only prayed rote prayers. The thought of talking to God in her own words in front of others made her sick. But she didn't give in to her fears and in time she conquered them. On the last day of class she gave me a big bear hug and whispered in my ear, "Thank you for teaching me to pray. It has made all the difference."

We usually end our study with a concert of prayer. God loves the beautiful sounds that echo through the room as the women bow their heads around their tables. Because it comes at the end, prayer is easily neglected. Don't let this become a habit. Make prayer a priority. But it won't matter how much time we allot if women don't pray.

How did we teach women to pray? Here are some suggestions. We eased them into it. For the first three weeks of class, we just took prayer requests. Each table had the freedom to handle prayer requests however they wanted. When the women arrived they wrote down their prayer requests. The leader took up the cards and read the requests. This method seemed to take less time than if every woman verbalized her own request. For the first three weeks, we passed out the cards and asked the women to pray for each other at home. We used the extra time building community.

On the fourth week, we streamlined the format to allow the leader time to teach a short workshop on how to pray together. A short testimony from an overcomer added to the effectiveness of this approach. We laid down parameters for conversational prayer and taught them about "popcorn" prayers—short, simple bursts of words to God.

We gave them freedom not to pray out loud but insisted that they join others silently in their hearts. We gently chided returning women who still weren't praying aloud and discussed the amazing promises and benefits of intercessory prayer. Then we prayed for about five minutes.

The leader opened with short words of praise, and then the women prayed for each other's needs. The leader had passed out the cards so nervous women simply prayed the request right off the card. Someone closed from the front. The next week, we extended the prayer time.

Sometimes a group member volunteered to e-mail weekly requests. Some groups asked a prayer captain to keep a journal of requests as well as answered prayer. What fun to read back over the requests and praise God.

We didn't browbeat women who didn't pray. We modeled prayer in everything we did. We thanked God for the awesome privilege of prayer. We found that our women became prayer warriors not out of compulsion but because they couldn't help it. Prayer works wonders. Teach women to pray and give them time to practice.

EMPLOY SURPRISE AND VARIETY

It's a sin to bore people with the Bible—or with Bible study! Don't lock yourself into the same format every week. Our Bible study lead team met after each study to plan the format for the next week. We asked God to reveal ways to drive his Word deep into the women's hearts with surprise and variety.

We didn't change it every week—only for a good reason. Here is a sample general format:

- Welcome and opening prayer
- Give-away incentive to be on time
- Small group time: take prayer requests, go over the lesson (about an hour)
- Announcements and service opportunities (five to ten minutes)
- Lecture (twenty-five to thirty minutes)
- Concert of prayer (ten minutes)

We begin on time and end on time—almost without exception. It's an integrity issue. We had scores of children waiting in the nursery, and we appreciated the Kids Klub's ministry. Dismissing on time kept us on good terms with our kids and their caregivers.

But within our time parameters, we had fun. Occasionally we added a video or other arts element wherever it was most effective. Sometimes it was in the lecture, if it illustrated a particular point. Other times it set up the lecture.

Sometimes we placed a special song or ceremony at the end. Occasionally we shortened the discussion time and tacked on a question the women hadn't seen to discuss after the lecture. A testimony might fit within the lecture or come at the beginning of the study to set up the theme.

On our last day of the year, we usually threw out the format and celebrated. We filled the time with all kinds of interesting surprises. We thanked our leaders, ate, prayed over summer requests, and introduced the next year's study. We sometimes asked the women to give us feedback on the year—either planned or spontaneous.

Have fun with the format and don't be afraid to try something new. It may bomb and then you won't do it again. But often it will be a special reminder to the women of how dear they are to you. Each week is another opportunity to enjoy an experience with Jesus.

PLAN TIGHT, BUT DON'T APPEAR STRUCTURED

I love structure. I like things where I can find them, and I like to know what's next. I like people who are on time, and I like things to go precisely as planned. I'm typical of many women of my generation. If you are like me, what I am about to say may seem silly, but hear me out. If you aren't attracting postmodern women, this could be why.

My daughters prefer a more relaxed approach and so do most of their friends. The postmodern women who lead and attend our studies want us to make every minute meaningful, but they don't like to feel rushed. They want to know that if there's a good reason to make a spontaneous change, we will.

Remember the bell? Young women hated it! For my first two years at IBC, we rang the bell. We rang it to let women know they had ten minutes left in their group time. I rang it when I was switching subjects as I led the concert of prayer from up front. I let them know they could wrap up what they were praying before we moved to another subject. I thought I was being considerate. They were annoyed.

In time they communicated their disdain for the bell. We threw it out. We still began and ended on time. And normally we followed the schedule. But if they needed a few more minutes in the group that day, we made a quick adjustment. And we didn't make an issue of time. It rolled along on schedule, but we didn't announce, "Five more minutes in your groups." Instead we said something like, "It looks like most of you are wrapping up. We'll get started on our announcements in a few minutes."

Actually, it is still highly structured. But we don't make a big deal of it. And we will flex if we need to. Women appreciate a more relaxed atmosphere—even though every minute is planned for maximum effect. It's just another way to make the experience pleasant in a 24/7 world.

Will any of these suggestions fit your ministry? If so, give them a try. The experience you create each week is a powerful tool to transform women. Not all women will be faithful. Studying the Scriptures is hard work. But for those who do, a great reward awaits them—an intimate relationship with Jesus, the great lover of their souls, and the blessing of a caring community. Knowing that you had a part in bringing them together is one of life's greatest joys!

A Woman of Influence
JACKIE HILL PERRY
by Lindsay Ann Nickens

The art of language is a unique, God-given craft honed precisely in St. Louis, Missouri native Jackie Hill Perry. A powerful rapper, poet, and writer, Jackie uses language as the conduit through which she is able to spread the message of the gospel. Jackie's albums provide a source of truth and gritty spiritual reality that is revealed through her own personal story.

As early as four years old, Jackie felt she ought to be a boy. This sexual identity grew after she was sexually abused when she was only five years old, so that she began mimicking boys by age six. Jackie, however, kept all of this silent until she began dating another young lady during her senior year of high school.

This decision threw Jackie into a lifestyle of lust and addiction until 2008, when God broke through her heart and revealed to Jackie her own sinfulness. She immediately decided to reject this lifestyle and follow passionately after the Lord, as she has done ever since.

Since her conversion, Jackie has devoted her life to shining the bright light of the gospel on a dark world seemingly void of hope. She began learning what biblical womanhood meant as she studied the life of Jesus in the Gospels and allowed her studies to rebuild her definition of what it meant to be a woman. In her albums, spoken-word poems, and article contributions to magazines, secular and Christian alike, Jackie is transparent about the redeeming work of Christ in her life as a self-described "ex-lesbian." She longs for the hurting and desperate to hear this impassioned cry: There is healing transformation in Jesus Christ, who loves you.

Today, Jackie lives with her husband, Preston Perry, and has two little girls, Eden and Autumn. She is the author of *Gay Girl, Good God* (B&H Books) and continues to speak into the lives of the broken.

CHAPTER 10

OFFER EXCITING EVENTS

A transforming women's ministry provides consistent opportunities for women to gather and grow spiritually, which is why it centers around regular study of God's Word. You will find, however, that women sometimes need to feel special, cared for, pampered. Periodic events provide a change of pace and opportunities for relationship and community and can be powerful tools to complement your ongoing ministries.

Events continue to offer a valuable on-ramp to your ministries' core elements. But feedback tells us that to be effective for all generations these events may need to be shorter and move from a programmatic thematic approach to a more organic feel focused on deep spirituality and authentic community connections. Keep these changes in mind as you read this chapter.

WENDI'S EXPERIENCE

Wendi was a successful lawyer, but she increasingly spent her evenings in front of a big screen TV with a rum and coke—make that, rum and cokes. Her husband of six years had encouraged her to take the promotion and move from their New England home to Dallas. His salary as an auto mechanic was a fraction of hers, but he liked his work and decided to stay until she was sure she liked the new job. The spark was flickering anyway.

The new job was challenging but internal conflict in the firm made the days tense. *Why all this competition?* Weekends she worked at home or sat on the couch missing her cat, Honey. *I'll send for her soon.*

Her neighbors Bonnie and Phil helped her hang a ceiling fan and made her a pie the day she moved in—coconut cream. "Best pie I've had in years," she told Bonnie, and it was true. *But who cooks anymore?* Nevertheless, the sense of being mothered lingered for months.

"A retreat—what's a retreat?" Wendi asked in response to Bonnie's invitation. "This one's just for women," explained Bonnie. "We get out of the city and into nature and just kick back for a couple days. You can ride horses, water ski, karaoke, or just relax with a good book. It would give you a chance to meet my friends. And we have a great speaker. I've heard her before. I'd love it if you'd come with me."

"I'll think about it," replied Wendi. She checked her calendar for that weekend. As usual, nothing. She liked Bonnie—a little weird, but genuine. *What could it hurt? I'll take my own car so I can escape if necessary.*

Wendi arrived late but Bonnie had been watching for her. At check-in she received a cloth-quilted name tag and a tote bag loaded with folders and goodies like earplugs, lotion, and chocolate. On the tote bag were the words, "Patterns of Our Lives." *What's the pattern of my life? No, I'm not here to think. I'm here to relax.*

The registration room fed into a huge room full of chairs—maybe four hundred. Around the walls hung dozens of quilts, and next to each quilt hung the story of the quilt and the woman whose hands had delicately stitched each piece of fabric to make a beautiful whole. Interwoven in the words were legacies of wise women devoted to family, friends, and faith. Their stories intrigued her.

Off to the dining hall to meet Bonnie's friends. Introductions, smiles, laughter. Wendi was so engrossed in their interaction she forgot the bland cafeteria food. She noticed a few other women like herself sitting in silence observing others, but most were caught up in stories and fun. Faint memories of Christy, her childhood friend. *We used to laugh like that. What happened?*

Women streamed into the quilt room, flopping down on red, yellow, or blue chair cushions. The first third of the room was red, the middle, yellow, and the back, blue. Wendi and Bonnie found two blue cushions. Being late had a price. But Linda, the emcee, introduced herself and asked each woman to sit on a different colored cushion each session. *Good, Bonnie and I will get to sit closer tomorrow.*

In the middle of Linda's announcements, Rachmaninoff's "Flight of the Bumble Bees" filled the room and four women in brightly colored bumblebee suits buzzed out of a twelve-foot hive on the stage. Linda pretended to be surprised. They introduced themselves as Queen Bee, Quilting Bee, Spelling Bee, and Busy Bee.

Queen Bee was obviously the leader. After a few minutes of clever slapstick humor the four buzzed off down the aisle to the roar of laughter. *Silly but clever.*

Linda introduced the worship leader and the speaker—both women belonged to Bonnie's church. Wendi wondered what church was like. She had never been in a church except for weddings and her grandfather's funeral.

Worship could only be described as an experience. Voices filled the room with praise. Bonnie showed her the words to the songs and she joined in as best she could. Why were these women singing with such intensity? Soon she too was lost in melody and rhythm. But who was this God they were praising?

The speaker opened with a prayer that sounded like a conversation—no big words, no flowery language—just simple affection. For the next thirty minutes, Wendi listened to her describe a sacred romance between herself and God.

The speaker was introduced to Christ in her twenties by her fiancé, and they both had decided to follow him. Within two years, they wearied of the corporate lifestyle and a marriage already on the rocks, so they left their jobs and traveled in a van for six months to focus on what God wanted for their lives.

They ended up in seminary, and now fifteen years later she was a Bible teacher. She spoke of a new joy and a transformed life. *Did they orchestrate this just for me? No, of course not. Look at all the other women here. Still. . . .*

The women split up into small groups all over the camp. Bonnie and Wendi were in the same group but everyone else was a stranger. They spent half an hour getting to know one another—two moms, a grandmother, three single women, one a paralegal.

Wendi connected with the paralegal, Susan, immediately. Although Susan worked for a law firm downtown and Wendi's firm was north of the city, her apartment was close to Wendi's rented house. Susan and Wendi talked for an hour after the small group while Bonnie visited with friends.

At the end of small group time, their leader gave each one a T-shirt—that fit each woman perfectly—with the same "patterns of life" logo as on her tote.

Snacks, games, loud music, karaoke in the barn, talking into the night. Wendi and Bonnie sat on their beds balancing plates of homemade chocolate chip cookies and cups of suisse mocha coffee.

They connected that night, and it was evident that Bonnie really enjoyed Wendi's sharp mind and sense of humor. Wendi opened up about her marriage, her drinking, and her restlessness. Bonnie listened intently but did not offer advice. Instead she told Wendi about her rebellious years and the way she wounded her Christian parents.

"How did you get over it?" asked Wendi.

"I fell in love with Jesus," answered Bonnie.

Restless sleep. Leisurely breakfast of pancakes and sausage. Back to the quilt room, now on the red cushions. The bumblebees buzzed. More worship. More Bible teaching. The Bible—*it's an ancient book,* thought Wendi—but this teacher brings it alive. Her words pierced Wendi's heart. *She's talking about me again.*

In the small group, the leader asked questions relating to the message. They grappled with tough issues—like why would God allow Susan's dad to die of cancer and what was the point of praying if God already knows what's going to happen. Wendi had never participated in a spiritual discussion before. The ideas about God and life fascinated her. Susan recommended a good book.

The afternoon was a smörgåsbord. Softball brought back memories of family reunions when mom and dad were together. Sweat, dirt, and ribbing the losers. After a shower, Bonnie suggested they attend a workshop on how to study the Bible. After years of undergraduate and law school Wendi knew how to study, but Bible study? How hard could it be? The class wasn't as easy as she thought, but she loved a challenge. And the teacher made it fun.

Saturday night several friends joined Wendi and Bonnie in their room. They rehashed the message and talked about their lives. Wendi listened. After lights out, she lay awake most of the night reflecting. These women loved life. They saw it as an adventure with God—a God who was their father and guide. And they loved each other. She observed over and over how they included everyone—even the *unlovable* women.

She wondered what they thought about her. Her ideas and life were so different from many of theirs—yet although she was among strangers, she felt somehow at home. They called themselves Christians, but they weren't the somber, judgmental Christians she'd seen portrayed in the media. Having Bonnie next door comforted Wendi, almost like a family member—the family she'd longed for but never experienced.

Bonnie had invited her to church and Bible study several times. *I think I'll go with her next time and see what kind of a church turns out people like this.*

If Wendi had been the only woman attending the retreat, it would have been worth the many hours spent planning and preparing. What was the purpose of this event?

THE PURPOSE FOR NONBELIEVERS

First, this event gave the Wendis of the world an opportunity to be exposed to a community of real Christians. For many postmodern women, an "in your face" kind of evangelism is counterproductive. Believers must overcome stereotyping from so much bad press. But living in the midst of authentic community for several days is a powerful tool to combat the bad press and cause women to reflect on God, their lives, and choices.

On Sunday morning at the retreat, the speaker presented the gospel and Wendi probably took her first communion among new family and friends. If not, she probably will after attending church and Bible study with Bonnie. Her marriage, her husband back home, her work, her extended family, maybe even future children—all will be affected by this event.

And Wendi is only one of many who attended.

THE PURPOSE FOR BELIEVERS

Of course, the majority of women attending are already believers. What's the purpose of the event for them? It is different for every woman. Some just need a weekend away from busy households and jobs to relax. Most have crises of some kind and interaction with the Word of God and concerned friends is invaluable.

Working moms and single parents, exhausted from overwhelming responsibilities, need a schedule change and a chance to spend a few hours relaxing by a lake.

Women seldom take time for themselves. Many are so busy taking care of others that they've never sung karaoke style or participated in an impromptu skit. Women normally in bed at ten find the energy to play games, laugh, and talk into the morning. They leave physically tired but surprised at their newfound zeal for life.

And most important, women do business with God. They make "fork in the road" decisions. They heal from wounds that have shackled them all their lives. They return determined to work on their marriages and conflicts. They go home passionate to serve God and encouraged to stretch in spite of their fears.

Was this event worth the hours invested? What do you think? And how would you create an event as welcoming and life-changing as this retreat? Let's look at the variety of events happening in women's ministries all over the country and then let's explore how to make it happen!

KINDS OF EVENTS

- Retreats—A day or two away at a camp, hotel, or the church for the women of the church and their friends
- Specialized retreats—For particular groups such as singles, working women, or moms
- Events on particular subjects such as prayer, community, worship, or solitude
- Events around food (breakfasts, brunches, luncheons, teas, dinners, desserts).
- Dinner theater—Are there women in your church interested or experienced in drama or music? Let them use their gifts to entertain and inspire.
- Craft fair—Raise money for women who work outside the home and offer affordable gifts.
- Faith-lift—Offer a day of workshops on various topics of interest to women.
- Training days—Do you need to train Bible teachers or small group leaders? Enlist a teacher to help equip leaders.
- Welcome event—Invite new women for a time of orientation to women's ministries and connecting with other newcomers.
- Mercy event—Sponsor a day ministering at a school, nursing home, hospital, or soup kitchen.

HOW TO MAKE IT HAPPEN

Determine Your Purpose

Why are you investing in this event? Determine your target audience. Does your event meet their needs? Don't continue an event that is no longer effective just because the women expect it. Surprise them with something new!

Include Variety

Does your ministry sponsor a healthy balance of different kinds of events? For example, does your event calendar include outreach, growth and development, and opportunities to serve? Are some events light and fun while others concentrate on serious spiritual issues? You don't necessarily need all these kinds of events every year, but don't overload the year with light events when the women need serious spiritual direction, and vice versa.

Recruit the Right Leader

A leader has influence and followers. She builds a team and inspires them to do the details. She needs vision to keep the big picture in mind and administrative gifts to delegate the details. The larger the event, the more critical her ability to give away the ministry.

Some women are sprinters, not distance runners. Use your distance leaders to head up ongoing ministries like Bible studies and prayer ministries. Enlist your sprinters for events. Women who travel periodically or have seasonal stresses can't always commit to weekly responsibilities. But they make great event coordinators.

Set the Budget

Events can be expensive. Will you need to cover your costs or can your church help out? Will women give scholarships to those who can't pay? If you stay off site, what kinds of accommodations will your women expect? Can you provide a variety of accommodations to allow *all* women to participate? Are there wealthy women in your church who might underwrite the cost? Nail down your resources and let your team know how much they have to spend.

A word to the smaller churches: bigger is not necessarily better. You have an advantage over the large churches—intimacy. Much of what goes into a large women's event is an attempt to develop and maintain the intimacy that a small group inherently enjoys. Be encouraged. You do not need a large budget or a large number of women to have a successful event. Do what you can with what you have. Some of the meticulous planning that goes into a large retreat like we described earlier probably won't be necessary for a smaller group of women.

Decide How Much You Can Pay and Choose Your Speaker

Speakers can be expensive and there is no standard. Whom should you choose? God has someone for you—often someone in your church or neighborhood. And she will be easier on your budget than will a "big name" speaker. Expect to pay a local speaker about $1,000 for a weekend, depending on her experience and credentials. If she speaks for only one session and she's just learning, $300 is adequate. And a woman from within your own church need not be paid at all, although a gift is appropriate. She's making her contribution to her church.

Even many local and in-house speakers should be booked a year ahead. Most limit their speaking engagements due to family or ministry obligations. Don't forget to make her experience memorable by providing a hostess, asking her how the team can pray, and thinking of special ways to express your appreciation.

She invests numerous hours preparing for the event. If she speaks several times, when she's not reviewing the upcoming message, she's with your women—and unless she's local, she'll probably never see them again. You can be sure she goes home exhausted—so do all you can to assist and support her.

Another option is securing a well-known author or speaker. Some are paid thousands of dollars and most expect to be generously compensated as well as airfare and expenses. A few ask for a percentage while others won't quote a fee. Some will take a love offering or allow you to decide on the amount.

Can you afford a big-name speaker? Is it worth what it will cost you? Many postmoderns are not as enamored with celebrity speakers as moderns. So consider your audience. If you really want this speaker, you may need to get on her waiting list, but patience and perseverance often pay off.

Decide How to Register the Women

A systematic, fair registration procedure squelches conflict and confusion. And the larger you are, the greater the necessity. Postmoderns and millennials expect an attractive, informative website or page on the church site with clear registration details. Plan on this method primarily, but decide if you also need paper brochures and registration cards.

TRAIN YOUR TEAM TO BE MINISTRY-MINDED

Teach your team that their specific tasks are only a small part of their calling. Ask them to complete the tasks ahead so they will be free to focus on their real role—to lavish the women with love and to make sure no one feels left out.

Why did Wendi feel special? Little things speak volumes. Her T-shirt fit. The extra effort to make the surroundings beautiful and comfortable said they cared. A wrapped gift under her chair and a chocolate on her pillow each night repeated the message. Women strategically placed to initiate conversation—especially to those alone—helped Wendi feel accepted.

However, teach the leaders to back off if they sense that a woman needs alone time. Help her feel safe participating but just as free to observe from the sidelines. Acquaint the women with the various activities available and then let them choose how they want to spend their time.

Plan Ahead

Why did the retreat impact Wendi? What happened in the year prior to the retreat to make it so meaningful? Why did she feel included and cherished? Here's a possible calendar for a Spring retreat and the methodology for the retreat that changed Wendi's life. Extract and adapt it to your events.

One to Two Years before the Retreat:
- Book the facility (camp, hotel, church).
- Decide on speaker and get on her calendar.

April (before the Retreat)
- Begin vision casting with lead team.
- Recruit retreat team (possible positions: coordinator, registration, decorations, hospitality).

- Distribute prayer calendar.

October
- Ask speaker for overview of messages.
- Finalize decor, coordinate with speaker's messages, and brainstorm creative uses.

November
- Create publicity for website, etc.
- Begin ongoing communication with camp or hotel.

January
- Publicize event and begin registration.
- Define and create decorations.
- Determine gifts for each woman and enlist a team to purchase or make them.

February
- Determine accommodations.
- Hold an event team dinner (status reports, worship, prayer, and great food).
- Make or order name tags, T-shirts, etc.
- Locate sound system and technician to work the event.

March
- Finalize schedules and details.
- Recruit emcees.
- Create notebooks, if needed.
- Wrap gifts.
- Send out notifications with room assignments and other information.

A Week before the Retreat (if Possible)
- Relocate to the retreat site with core leaders.
- Decorate, bond, practice, pray, and play.

Friday Morning before the Retreat
- Set up last-minute details.
- Check sound system.
- Prep greeters.
- An hour before women arrive—team prayer time with all leaders and speakers

As Women Arrive
- Position all leaders at registration and later at dinner, relaxed and available to interact and welcome women.
- Women at registration table alert and ready to identify a woman who is alone, informally assign a caretaker
- Dorm mothers in each dorm also alert to help women connect with others

During the Retreat
- Don't miss opportunities to connect.
- Execute your task.
- Help work out the kinks.

After the Retreat
- Clean up, break camp, and praise God!

Creative, innovative events add zest to your year and give women entry points into your ministry. Often after a positive experience at an event, a woman will join your ongoing ministries—and they often build on the event. In addition, events break the routine with special times that women write on their calendars with anticipation. Make your events worthy and use them to transform lives.

Chapter 11

ADD OTHER MINISTRIES WISELY

After your Bible study is established, how do you add other ministries? Let's look at the process and then at a list of potential ministries to consider.

THE PROCESS

Cynthia was a devoted wife and mother of five children. The leaders loved her insight in leader's group. Her answers inspired us and made us think. But her real passion was ministry to moms. How do I know? Here's what happened.

Many young families attend our church. As a mother, I know the stress during those first years. I know moms need training and encouragement. After our Bible study was established, I began to pray for a moms' ministry. Notice that I did not run out and start one. My calling was to cast vision, recruit, equip, train, teach, and lead. Somewhere in our church was a woman burning with a desire to minister to moms.

During Bible study I often joined table discussions to connect with women. That morning I *just happened* to sit at Cynthia's table. One of the application questions asked, "If you could do any significant work for Christ in your church, family, or community, what would that work be? What can make your dream a reality?"

The women shared their dreams and then Cynthia added, "I have always wanted to start a ministry to moms." She explained why, and her words were pregnant with excitement. I shot up a word of gratitude to God. And after the study I was on her like cops on Krispy Kremes.

I never thought of asking her because of her other responsibilities. I knew she was capable but I wasn't sure the timing was right. God knew my heart and hers, and he made his choice clear. She prayed for God's direction and he confirmed that he wanted her to lead this ministry.

We met and prayed as she researched other moms' ministries. She advertised it as a ministry to mothers of young children rather than "young mothers of children" in sensitivity to new moms in their thirties and forties. She devised a structure and built a team of four, delegating each arm of the ministry to one of them. I asked them to pick a meeting time that would not compete with Bible study. They chose to gather once a month in the evening when dads were available to watch kids.

Within several months, Cynthia had her calendar and speakers in place. The ministry exceeded my expectations. I attended the first three months and then attended sporadically. They didn't need me. I went for my own enjoyment when I could. When invited to speak, I accepted with pleasure. I loved watching these women birth and nurture this ministry to our moms.

I knew we would lose Cynthia as a Bible study leader, but she still attended faithfully. The moms' ministry was her calling. Even when she became pregnant with her fifth child, the leadership was so strong that they kept it going during her leave of absence.

Are new ministries always birthed with such ease? No, but they can be, when you follow some simple guidelines.

Discern a Leader's Readiness
(or How to Turn Someone Down Graciously)

God won't always plop the leader in your lap like he did with Cynthia. But often he will make his choice clear. As women are transformed through the Bible study, they hear God calling them to serve. I challenged them constantly to step out and stretch. When they did, they took giant leaps in their spiritual growth.

Here's how the process unfolded:

As a result of a woman's desire to serve, she would come to my office and tells me that God wanted her to start a new ministry. Often, he did—but sometimes she wasn't ready. I had to discern which. And if she wasn't ready, I wanted to help her see this for herself. My goal—and yours—was not to push my agenda on her, but to love her. We must let our women know that *they* matter to us more than our plans and schedules do.

When a woman expressed her desire to start a new ministry, I asked her to explain her vision. As she did so, I was asking God for wisdom. If she was active in women's ministry, I had the opportunity to observe her. If not, I was at a disadvantage.

QUESTIONS TO CONSIDER

I asked God to show me whether she was mature enough to lead others, to handle conflict, and to follow through. If she wasn't, guess who had to step in? And guess who didn't have the time?

I also considered whether women needed this ministry right then. Did it fall under the umbrella of our women's ministry vision? Or should I send her to another pastor where her idea was a better fit? Was this where we wanted to use our resources?

I gently asked her why she believed God was leading her. I tried to identify her motives. Was she starving for attention and thought by leading a ministry others would admire her? Was there a tragedy or abuse in her own life with which she still had not dealt? Or was her primary motivation to minister to others and bring glory to God?

I also probed to learn if she had any experience leading. Had she organized a home, managed a business, or overseen a grocery co-op? Could she delegate and lead others? Did she have any idea how to make the ministry happen?

WHAT NEXT?

If I sensed this was God's doing, I would communicate my support and ask her to bring me a proposal to submit to the women's lead team. We talked generalities of how and when. And we prayed for God's direction and enablement. This is how ministries are birthed, and it was an honor to be part of the process.

If I was unsure, I would not communicate my support of the project, but neither would I tell her of my doubts. I affirmed her personally and prayed for her. I also asked her to bring me a proposal. I found that if she was not ready, it became clear when she tried to write the proposal. Either I never heard from her again or she returned realizing that this was not the time.

If she returned with a well-written proposal, we talked about details such as a calendar and team building. I asked God for red flags. Was she willing to work with others, or was she a one-woman show? We didn't need mavericks. If it still looked good, I took the proposal to the next lead team meeting for approval. If the lead team confirmed the idea, I often asked her to attend the next lead team meeting as my guest where she could share her vision and answer questions.

I watched to see how she interacted with other team members. Did she seem excited about their ministries? Did she understand that her ministry would be part of a bigger picture? Or was she restless when the attention moved to others? Clues emerged as I observed her with the lead team members. These clues helped us know if she was God's choice to oversee his work.

Notice that because the lead team met monthly, we considered this project for several months. The timing was intentional. I wanted to know if her passion was just a flash in the pan or a desire that would continue to burn over time. We met several times. I saw her in different situations to assess her character and background. If we believed God wanted this ministry as part of what we offered women, and if she was still excited about the project and so were we, we got serious.

UNDERGIRD HER WITH RESOURCES

What does she need to make it happen? money? leaders? a place to meet? publicity? Whatever it is, be ready to help all you can. Don't ask someone to join your ministry and then fail to give her what she needs.

Usually a new ministry launches before we can put it in the budget. But part of enlisting support is getting the approval of lead pastors. Ask them to provide whatever resources they can, including money. But don't go to them until you have taken the steps that we just described.

If the resources are not available, adjust our kickoff accordingly. Understand it is not God's timing and wait. But when it all comes together, move ahead.

DON'T MICROMANAGE, BUT MONITOR PROGRESS

Insightful leaders know how much to help. Each leader needs something different.

Cynthia

Cynthia was gifted and capable, but young. She didn't have extensive experience. So I met with her several times as she began. I asked her to report what she learned about other moms' ministries. I attended the first leader's dinner meeting in her home.

As I worked with her, it became evident that she didn't need help. She was organized, efficient, and wise beyond her years. I stepped back in awe and told her often that she was doing a great job! After one gathering, I told her she could lead a full-blown women's ministry one day—and I meant it. If she wants to, she will. However, even though she was capable, I didn't know that initially. So I followed from a distance for a while, until I was sure I could let her go.

Andi

My assistance to Andi was different. She and I worked together in Bible studies before either of us came to IBC. She was wise and godly, and I knew if she tackled a project, it would be done well. I had seen her work. When she consented to build a mercy ministry for us, I knew that she knew how.

We met once. She returned with a proposal that would jump-start a small company. I went to work on the resources. In a month, she had five co-captains and teams under them in process. She divided the ministry into meals for the sick, housecleaning, hospital visitation, special needs, and handyman help. The first year she enlisted four hundred volunteers and the ministry went church-wide.

I knew that Andi would inform me of any imperative issues. I did not need to walk beside her at the beginning. I didn't even follow from a distance. There was no need.

Celeste

Celeste felt led by God to start a widows' ministry in my former church. She was responding to a definite need. Many widows attended the church, but nothing existed to bring them together or serve them. Celeste had a heart for widows, but she was terrified. She had never led anything and lacked confidence.

I walked with her every step of the way for two years. I showed her how to organize the ministry. I took her to the church secretary and showed her how to get an event on the church calendar. At first I led the planning meetings and attended every event.

But gradually, I gave over the reins of the ministry to her. She would lead part of the meetings and I would lead the other part. Then later I would attend but she would lead. Finally she did it all herself. What a blessing to see her grow! She became a gracious leader who brought joy into many widows' lives. It was worth the investment.

Always count the cost. Be sure you can make an investment without neglecting your other responsibilities.

Supervise each woman depending on her experience and abilities. Your goal is to hand off the ministry as soon as possible. Seldom involve yourself in the details. Women with this kind of vision will name their ministry, build their own teams, and supervise the details—with the exception of a Celeste at first. They dream their own dreams and then entrust those dreams to God.

Your role is to encourage and guide. If their creative ideas fizzle, you are there to help get them back on their feet. If they veer from the initial vision, direct them back. When the ministry flourishes, they receive credit—which they will learn to give back to God.

When you refuse to micromanage, the ministry becomes theirs. Give them the responsibility and the authority. Of course, you are ultimately accountable. Therefore, be careful not to put a woman in leadership before she is ready. And monitor everyone's progress as best you can.

It's risky to unleash passionate women to do ministry that will reflect on you. But it's worth the risk. Because it is the way women learn what God can do through them. One day you will die or retire, and one of them will continue the work. Praise God! Isn't that what ministry is all about anyway?

Team Building

By now you recognize our passion for doing ministry as a team. The leaders of your added ministries will also need to know how to build their own teams. Insist on it. Even if your church is small, your new leaders will need teammates (perhaps just one or two at the beginning) to share the load. Also, teach them how to recognize a possible replacement. For more information on team building, see chapter 4.

Potential Ministries to Consider

Don't be pressured into adding new ministries—especially if you are a small church. Add them if it fits and the time is right. If a woman had wanted to start a widows' ministry at IBC, I would have declined.

Do I believe widows aren't worthy of a ministry? Not at all. But only a handful of widows attend IBC. Simpler ways exist to support them rather than creating a full-blown ministry just for them. However, in my former church, there were many widows. Not only did I encourage Celeste to plant the ministry, I invested many hours myself.

If a woman had asked to begin a ministry to single moms, I would also have declined. Many single moms attended our church. And many of them were active in our Bible studies. Why then would I resist beginning a single moms' ministry? Because Bob, our adult education pastor, sponsored a dynamic single parents class that, once a month, organized a single parents' night out and treated the kids to fun, food, and fellowship at the church. If a woman came to me with a passion to minister to single moms, I would send her to Bob. Cooperate—don't compete!

A stellar women's ministry focuses on people, not programs. If the people are engaged in a transforming relationship with Jesus and are learning his Word, then think about adding other ministries as the Lord leads. Remember: the hub of the wheel is Bible study. All other ministries are the spokes.

However, one exception is prayer. Prayer is a pillar of the Bible study, but I recommend you develop a more extensive prayer ministry.

Here is a list of other options:

Ministry to Specific Groups

Moms, widows, single moms, working women, abortion recovery, divorce recovery, moms of children with special needs, infertility, blended families, families fighting drugs, cancer survivors, nursing home

Service Opportunities

Meals for new moms and the sick, hospital visitation, prison ministry, financial counseling, crisis pregnancy, inner-city missions, world missions, car ministry, food pantry, clothes closet, welcoming new women, office assistance, tutoring

Events

Retreats, conferences, workshops, dinners, lunches, brunches, teas, intramural sports, aerobics, out of town trips, museums, art galleries, theater

It may sound like we are against beginning new ministries. Not true. We supported all kinds of ministries. We are simply cautioning you to be wise with your resources—especially if you are a small church. You can't do everything well.

But if a passionate woman wants to plant a ministry that you and your lead team believe is needed, go for it. Over time women will ask to start all kinds of ministries. Most will enrich your women's lives and give them places to use their gifts. These ministries will meet a felt need and fit within the scope of your vision. As you expand your borders, more and more women will benefit.

A Woman of Influence
JULIE WATERS
by Amanda Sherzer

"**What will the next chapter** of my life look like?" attorney Julie Waters wondered when she moved to Texas in 2009. Little did she know she stood on the cusp of God igniting a new passion in her heart.

During a mission trip to the Middle East, he opened her eyes to the oppression of sex trafficking. Upon returning stateside, she discovered her home of Houston was a leading hub of this injustice. Julie couldn't look away. The modern-day slavery she confronted overseas existed in her own backyard, and Julie knew God wanted to use her to free those in bondage .

She followed God's lead by founding *Free the Captives*, a non-profit that combats the exploitation and sex trafficking of Houston's youth. She devotes her life to serving victims of trafficking as she helps them heal, equips them for their futures, and shows them Christ's love.

Julie and her team work closely with law enforcement to rescue victims between the ages of twelve and eighteen. Many of these girls grew up in poverty-stricken and fatherless homes with little affection. They instead found love with manipulative men who coerced or forced them into prostitution. This abuse shredded their self-esteem and shrouded them with shame. Their hearts grew so traumatized they could not fathom escape from the streets existed.

Free the Captives walks alongside these girls *for years* as they work and pray for the deep wounds to heal. They provide the girls with one-on-one mentoring and a weekly support group where the girls share their similar experiences and realize, sometimes for the first time, they are not alone. Julie and her team also run a summer job program in which the girls produce 4,000 candles to sell while learning life skills, such as how to write a resume and create a budget. Julie said the program makes a huge difference as "it shows the girls what they are capable of and gives them a glimpse of what their future could be like."

Throughout it all, Julie prays for the power of Christ to work in these girls' hearts, because without him, they will not experience full healing. God graciously responds to these prayers. Julie shared, "The girls have a hunger for God. They long to know God is with them and that there is something bigger than what has happened to them."

Julie strives to protect other girls from the trauma of trafficking. She speaks to at-risk girls about the dangers of trafficking to prevent them from walking down the wrong road. She educates the community about trafficking through *Free the Captives*'s trainings and annual conference. And she advocates to stop men from purchasing sex and fueling the trafficking industry.

Julie, a 2016 Dallas Theological Seminary graduate, praises the school for helping her to strengthen *Free the Captives*. She immediately applied the lessons she learned in seminary to her organization, enabling her to build it into a thriving non-profit which has served over four hundred girls since its inception. Many of these girls have found careers, achieved academically, and grown in their relationships with God . . . all thanks to Julie following God's call years ago.

Julie encourages other believers to walk in obedience and put God first. "Be open and flexible," she advises, "you might be surprised where God is leading you."

CHAPTER 12

PREPARE FOR AND SURVIVE CONFLICT

I'm *so sorry,* but I must ask you to step down from the board until we sort all this out." I (Sue) spoke gently, but still Angela's blue eyes brimmed with tears. Then she forced them back and declared, "No, I'll resign. I've had it! Ministry isn't supposed to be like this."

You're right, I agreed silently. It sure isn't.

Serving as women's ministry director was usually my life's delight—but that day was anything but delightful. I had dreaded our meeting, especially as I remembered Angela's two years of wholehearted service.

But her outspoken disagreement with several staff members and her continuous, public undercutting of authority made this day inevitable. Angela and her family left the church. What a waste. What a loss.

IT'S MORE COMMON THAN YOU THINK

Stay in ministry long enough and you will encounter conflict. It's my least favorite part of the job. But it's reality. Fortunately I would not describe my ministry years as full of conflict, but often—too often—conflicts have arisen. Many have been minor, but others have threatened the life of the ministry. Here's what happened to me in the early 1990s.

"You are holding women's hands to hell."

Sylvia glared at me across the table. She accused me of false teaching before the executive pastor and several other staff members. We were teachers of unrelated Bible studies in the same church, and many of her former students were in my classes.

"You teach women *cheap grace,*" she accused. "You must be stopped."

For a year, she attempted to destroy my ministry and reputation. After multiple meetings with pastors, in which I was forced to defend my theology, the pastor dismissed the accusation as untrue and asked us to coexist in harmony.

However, factions were birthed. One of her followers repeatedly slandered me. Sylvia also paid a high price. Month after month, the mudslinging continued. The executive pastor's gag order mandated that I not defend myself. So I learned to trust God as my advocate. But I wondered if my integrity would ever be restored.

As word of the conflict seeped out over that year, women went on the offensive for both of us. Some were deeply wounded and others left the church without ever understanding what really happened. During those dark days, we witnessed the results of out-of-control conflict.

My accuser continued to say, "This isn't personal." But if it involves people, it's personal. Conflict handled badly damages people. I recall days of weeping, and I'm sure other women do too.

But I also experienced God's faithfulness. And I learned to focus on pleasing God instead of people. These were valuable lessons that equipped me for future ministry. We all made mistakes. There were no winners—and God was dishonored. Mine is an extreme example, but all leaders will face conflict in some form. Learn from my experience!

BE INTENTIONAL

I promised God that if I ever had the privilege of serving him again, I would study how to resolve conflict biblically and I would help others learn to be skilled peace-makers. Now as a seminary professor, I have the opportunity to train future ministers to expect and prepare for conflict. I've kept that promise.

We also wrote a book to address ways women engage in conflict, entitled *Leading Women Who Wound: Strategies for an Effective Ministry* (Kregel Publications, 2009).

Below are some of the book's highlights:

- Consider asking your leaders to sign a covenant promising that they will deal with disputes according to Matthew 18:15–17 (see Appendix D for Conflict Resolution Covenant).

- Model peace-making skills yourself. If a woman says, "I am so angry about the way Jane treated me at the meeting," I look her in the eye and ask, "Have you talked to Jane about this?" Then I explain that Jesus gave us directives to help us work through hurts and disagreements. And I strongly suggest that she work this out with Jane instead of talking to me.

- Whether you mediate a dispute or are a party to the conflict, you'll never forget the tense, exhausting hours of resolving conflict—especially if the problem is mishandled initially.

  » One member of a leadership team that was formed to improve a particular ministry didn't like some of the proposed changes and met secretly with the pastor, maligning the ministry. The leadership team felt betrayed, and the ministry was temporarily sidetracked.

  » A Bible study planning committee could not agree on next year's curriculum, expressing its foundational differences in constant, petty skirmishes. The next year, many of the leaders resigned.

  » In a Bible class, two people embroiled in a theological discussion over the sovereignty of God and free will ended their debate by taking swings at each other. Imagine trying to explain that to visitors!

CAUSES AND COMPLEXITY

Conflicts vary in complexity. Some happen between those who serve and those being served. At other times those serving together as leaders cannot agree. Then there may be friction between ministries within a church.

Conflicts may stem from doctrinal differences, personality clashes, or different ministry philosophies, styles, and traditions. Typically, each party is sure it is on a mission from God and that he is on their side.

CAN CONFLICT BE PREVENTED?

Sometimes I see disagreements resolved graciously and the parties grow from the experience. Just as often, it ends like Angela's case or mine—in disaster. The wounded limp away, often never to serve again. The world hears one more account of how Christians "just can't get along." It's time to get serious about managing conflict *before* it's out of control. We need to recognize the early warning signs of conflict and understand how to address it when it erupts. Certain biblical principles should be a part of our basic training.

WHAT JESUS SAYS

One of the most familiar passages on resolving conflict is Matthew 18:15–17. Jesus prepared his disciples and us with these words that are hard to obey, and we ignore them to our peril. Verse 15 says, "If your brother or sister sins, go and point out their fault, just between the two of you. If they listen to you, you have won them over."

Step One: Go and Show

First, note that there are two parties in the conflict: the offender and the offended. Both are assumed to be Christians, as indicated by the Greek term *adelphos*, translated brother or sister. Jesus instructs the offended to be the initiator in the peace process. If you are wounded, *you* are to go to the one who hurt you.

Notice also that the offense is termed a sin. What constitutes a sin? Sins listed in the Bible include sexual immorality, debauchery, coarse joking, theft, drunkenness, idolatry, witchcraft, hatred, discord, jealousy, rage, anger, selfish ambition, envy, bitterness, slander, gossip, quarreling, and pride (cf. Gal. 5:19–21; Eph. 4:31; 2 Cor. 12:20). Is the offense truly a sin, or could it lead to sin? Are you evaluating an action you have observed or a heart attitude you suspect? Are you making assumptions that may or may not be true?

Also, you must decide if you can overlook this offense. "A person's wisdom yields patience; it is to one's glory to overlook an offense" (Prov. 19:11). Ask yourself, "Can I chalk this up to a bad day? Can I interact with my offender without this offense coloring our relationship?" If you can, forget it! If you can't, you should initiate a meeting with your offender to offset problems later.

Many people would prefer to resign from their commitments rather than discuss the conflict openly with their offender. The thought of expressing the hurt face to face is ranked with having a root canal or giving a political speech to an audience of opponents—no one looks forward to the experience. There is a possibility of greater misunderstanding and even rejection. But with prayer and Christ-like love, you may leave the meeting with a more intimate, authentic friend than before.

The Principle of Containment

"Just between the two of you . . ."

Jesus limits the first meeting to the two parties—and no one else should know about the conflict. When I am hurt, the first thing I want to do is call my closest friends or corner my spouse and unload. I may try to fool myself into believing that I am doing this to gain wisdom or convince myself I need a sounding board. Sometimes that is true, but more often, I want to give my listener the gift of carrying the offense with me. Unfortunately, if the conflict is resolved, my listener, who was not privy to the peace process, may continue to carry the offense long after my offender and I have laid it down.

Step Two: Take Witnesses

> But if they will not listen, take one or two others along, so that "every matter may be established by the testimony of two or three witnesses" (Matt. 18:16).

Jesus says that if the first meeting is unfruitful, the offended party is responsible to call a second meeting and invite witnesses. Who are these witnesses? In this verse, Jesus quotes Deuteronomy 19:15. According to Mosaic Law, when an accusation was made, witnesses were to tell any related truth. A witness joins the process to testify to the truth or falsehood of the offender's account and to help the two parties see the conflict honestly. Jesus is asking those who may have insight concerning the offense to join the parties and help sort out relevant details.

I am astounded at how differently Christians view events, actions, attitudes, and even the Christian life. Witnesses can serve as catalysts to bring about truth and a joyful resolution. But there are no guarantees.

Step Three: Take It to the Church

> If they still refuse to listen, tell it to the church (Matt. 18:17).

If Jesus's instructions have been followed, no more than five people know of the conflict. Now they must "tell it to the church." What does Jesus mean?

When two hardworking, respected women could not settle their dispute in the church at Philippi, Paul placed the issue squarely in the laps of the leadership. "I plead with Euodia and I plead with Syntyche to be of the same mind in the Lord. Yes, and I ask you, my true companion, help these women since they have contended at my side in the cause of the gospel . . ." (Phil. 4:2–3).

Whomever God has placed in authority over you in the church must now take charge. Courtesy dictates that all parties are heard at the same time, and godly people follow the directives of their leaders. Then we can rest in the assurance that the outcome will ultimately be God's best for us.

What blessings can we experience as we learn the skill and art of peacemaking? Through conflict, we can see God at work in issues and relationships; we can learn more about his character and faithfulness as well as more about ourselves. Conflict resolution can mature and equip us. It can prepare us to minister in the real world. Although we often tend to view conflict negatively, Jesus said, "Blessed are the peacemakers, for they will be called children of God" (Matt. 5:9).

For a thorough treatment of women's conflict styles and strategies to become effective peacemakers while leading women, digest *Leading Women Who Wound*.[33]

CHAPTER 13

MINISTERING WITH MEN

The staff of Ridgeway Community Church sat in senior pastor Chip's office in silence. A tiny tear rolled down Nancy's cheek, and although the four men pretended not to notice, they all saw it and their conversation quit cold as a result.

All four men had welcomed Nancy as women's ministry director a year earlier. They valued her insight and appreciated her stellar ministry. They saw the results in the lives of their wives and were grateful.

Nancy sat quietly through most of the staff meetings, speaking up occasionally when the conversation concerned her ministry. The men had become accustomed to her presence, carrying on with their usual bantering and almost forgetting she was there. But now this—a tear.

They had gathered to hammer out next year's calendar. Nancy had reserved the second Thursday in December almost a year before for the annual women's Christmas dinner. The date aligned with their sought-after speaker's calendar, and the women were ecstatic. They had been trying to bring her in for three years.

But Greg, the missions pastor, had scheduled that weekend for the missions conference, forgetting to inform Chip's assistant, the keeper of the calendar. Greg vied for the calendar date as if he were out to win a competitive tennis match. He raised his voice in a strong, heated tone, used sarcasm, and pounded the table once with his fist.

Greg often reacted this way, and the other men joined in the game. They jostled each other, joked, and jeered to make their point—and then went out to lunch together. But Nancy wouldn't compete. The result—a tear in staff meeting! The men were dismayed and perplexed.

How Will Women Change the Staff?

Men and women often communicate differently. In many ministries women have joined formerly all-male staffs, and most men welcome them. But when someone who often communicates differently joins the staff, everyone must adjust. The dynamic of staff interaction is affected.

Whether one woman or ten participate on staff, they bring change—and often a presence and a tone that benefits the ministry. After all, churches are full of females. A woman's influence in the inner workings of staff most often results in decisions that woo women to Christ and make the environment more favorable to their flourishing.

How will a woman's presence affect the staff meeting? What adjustments should men make? We observed that the men on staff at Ridgeway Community Church continued to interact the way they always had before Nancy joined them. How was Nancy feeling during their meetings?

She seldom participated because their interaction was decidedly male. Their teasing sometimes bordered on ridicule. Their playful, competitive bantering made her uncomfortable. She set a softer, gentler tone in her women's team meetings. Should the men change the way they relate to each other because a woman joined the team? Yes and no.

Both Need to Adapt

Certainly Greg was insensitive toward Nancy in his attempts to win the calendar war. But neither can Nancy expect Greg to interact with her the way most women would. When men and women are working together for the good of the church and God's glory, both must adapt!

Nancy must learn to assert herself in the meetings when she believes she needs to speak up. Please don't misunderstand. Her tone should be gracious. She would be wise to think through her requests beforehand and present them clearly. She must be careful not to overreact or take personally the men's comments when no offense was intended. Whining, excessive talking, and crying is counterproductive.

On the other hand, men should remember that a woman is among them, respect her presence, and make appropriate changes. Competitive bantering and shoulder punching may be out of place. Give and take on both sides will result in a united staff that supports and trusts each other. The church will benefit as the congregation observes a beautiful picture of men and women serving God together in harmony. Marriages will be strengthened and gender issues addressed.

MOST MEN WELCOME WOMEN ON STAFF, BUT . . .

Many churches welcome women on staff and work hard to accommodate and value them. Steve Roese, IBC's executive pastor, asked Sue regularly what she needed to fulfill her call as women's pastor. His door was always open when she sought direction or even a listening ear. He hired a graphic artist to upgrade the study guide she wrote for the Bible classes. Working with Steve and men like him was a joy.

And in the majority of churches where women serve, men support them wholeheartedly. But some men resist the changes women bring when they join staff. For a variety of reasons we will examine, they don't want you ministering with them. What do you do if you believe God has called you to serve with resistant men?

SURVIVE MEN WHO DON'T VALUE YOU

Darlene's Story

"I'll never have a woman on my staff," stated the senior pastor. Actually the secretaries and the financial officer were women. But Darlene knew what he meant—he would never hire her in a pastoral role.

The comment cut because she had been serving in a pastoral role for five years. She taught the women's Bible study and directed the women's ministry. She counseled women daily. She was one of the founders and loved the women dearly. However, she wasn't on staff, nor was she compensated financially although some weeks she worked over fifty hours. Darlene had never attended a staff meeting. She simply wasn't included in the inner workings of the church.

She prayed from the beginning that the church leaders would value her efforts so that women's ministry could earn enough credibility to be included as part of the staff. Darlene did not expect that she would be the woman they brought on staff—although she would have loved to join the team. But she knew from the pastor's comment that it would never happen.

However, Darlene also knew God had called her to love, teach, and train the women. She ministered there for another three years until God removed her and sent her to a church where she enjoyed staff support and was well paid. The year Darlene left, God withdrew several influential women from the church, women's ministries floundered, and within a year the church had hired a paid director of women's ministries. God was working.

It's Part of Ministry

Is Darlene the only woman ever wounded by a man in ministry? No! And if you serve with men long enough, you may get hurt. I (Sue) often hear from women with similar stories.

A children's ministry director sat in my office bewildered. The all-male staff excluded her from staff meetings and the yearly staff retreat. She asked if she was overreacting and if not, how to convince them to involve her for the sake of her ministry and the church at large.

Why do some men oppose partnering with women in ministry? And if God calls you into a setting where you are not valued, how should you respond? Let's explore these questions.

WHY DO SOME MEN RESIST WOMEN IN MINISTRY?

Imagine working with a sixty-eight-year-old pastor who believes that 1 Timothy 2 prohibits women from all leadership positions in the church, thinks that the working mother was a disgrace to God, and labels all women as untrustworthy gossips because he remembers one who forty years ago had criticized one of his sermons. Sound like the ideal boss?

Thankfully, this fellow is fictitious! We created him to highlight the obstacles that often prevent some men from accepting women as partners in ministry: tradition, their view of what the Scriptures teach regarding women's roles in the church, irrational fears, and the possibility of negative experiences from the past. Any or all of these issues may color a male pastor's perspective on working with women.

Tradition

Thirty years ago, a female staff member on the church payroll was likely to be the secretary or the organist. Pastoral positions were traditionally reserved for men. However, since the 1980s, women's ministry positions are common on large church staffs. And in more small churches, women are added as finances allow.

The change is evident in the seminaries as well. DTS, a theologically conservative school, began allowing women to study for a degree in 1976. When Sue attended from 1985 to 1989, women made up 12 percent of the student body. At the time, women were discouraged from pursuing a master of theology (ThM), the four-year program designed to train pastors. Yet when Kelley began her studies in 1994, she was encouraged to earn her ThM because its coursework aligned with her goals better than any of the two-year programs. And by the time she graduated in 2000, women constituted over 25 percent of the student body. Today the number is closer to 40 percent. These numbers reflect an administration willing to adapt to the changing times by acknowledging the growing need for and benefit of training women to do the work of ministry.

Unfortunately, many men who lead *traditional* churches refuse to change. They enjoy a "good ole boys network" where a woman doesn't fit. Some male pastors don't want to include women and probably never will. Women whom God calls to minister there must face that fact and choose to serve without resentment. They will need a right heart attitude that will honor God and help them survive.

However difficult, personal bias is not the primary obstacle women face. Most pastors think their opinions reflect God's will as revealed in Scripture.

Scripture

Why are some people so opposed to women serving on pastoral staffs? Ask most of them, and they'll point to a Bible passage or two to support their position. What *does* the Bible teach about the role of women in ministry? Bible scholars disagree.

If you lead women, you must understand the various views on the role of women in the church. We recommend several books that explain the spectrum of perspectives from traditional to egalitarian.

1. *Neither Complementarian nor Egalitarian: A Kingdom Corrective to the Evangelical Gender Debate*, Michelle Lee-Barnewall

2. *Men and Women in the Church: Building Consensus on Christian Leadership*, Sarah Sumner
3. *Man and Woman, One in Christ: An Exegetical and Theological Study of Paul's Letters*, Philip B. Payne
4. *Women and Men in Ministry: A Complementary Perspective*, Robert Saucy and Judy TenElshof

Titus 2

So what *is* clear in the Bible regarding women in ministry? Titus 2:3–5 presents irrefutable evidence that the Bible allows women—even more, it commands them—to minister to other women and children.

Elizabeth Inrig, in her book *Release Your Potential,* offers this reminder to the women and men in church leadership.

> Women committed to becoming fully developed Christ followers in the spirit of Titus 2:3–5 hold in their hands and hearts an enormous amount of spiritual power. It is a privilege denied men. It is the power to convince a watching world that God's purposes for men and women to function together in the church reflect the glorious interdependence of the Holy Trinity. . . . The power comes when women take up the task of teaching the next generation of women to know and obey God's Word (Titus 2:3–5).[34]

Harmony. It's the sound produced when each instrument in an orchestra performs its intended role, the notes coming together to create a harmonious blend of music. So it should be in the church.

But how will this look in an individual church? Will the woman coordinating or directing such woman-to-woman ministry be acknowledged and supported by the church leadership? Will she be invited to join the staff in an official capacity? Each church must decide how much value it places on ministry to women.

Such change is difficult for some. It is made all the harder when unfounded fears and false assumptions about women obscure some men's minds.

Fear

Why are some men afraid to include women? They fear women in ministry will lead to moral failure.

Every person in leadership faces temptations to use that position for their own benefit. Some male pastors—too many—have abused their position of spiritual leadership through sexual misconduct. The reports have been heartbreaking. Some male church leaders fear that having women on staff would increase the potential for their own moral failure. If they work closely together, the argument goes, they may find themselves attracted to one another and tempted sexually.

We have addressed this issue extensively in our book *Mixed Ministry: Working Together as Brothers and Sisters in an Oversexed Society*. Leaders who are spiritually and emotionally mature can—and must—partner together effectively as they serve the church. This is true of both men and women. The church needs both in leadership in order to shepherd the church in all of her diversity.

And, on a practical note, having a woman on staff to share the counseling load will help alleviate uncomfortable situations in which male pastors may find themselves. Let the women leaders counsel the women who come for help.

Paul instructed Titus to delegate women's ministry to women—and this is a key reason. It just makes good sense. Men who fear to work on staff with women should consider this benefit.

HOW DO YOU RESPOND WHEN YOU AREN'T VALUED?

Respond with Grace

We all need God's grace! We all have blind spots. Men who don't value women are sinners. Prejudice against any people group is a sin (see James 2:9). But women who respond with animosity are sinners too. If we understand the source of the sin, we are more inclined to give grace.

There are many reasons men resent women. Some men who fear or dislike women have unresolved issues rooted deep in past experiences. Some cling to traditions passed on from men they respected growing up.

Particular personality types gravitate to power. These men naturally hold theological positions that feed their desire to dominate. They find it difficult to change unless they are challenged to examine their views—usually by other men. Their sin against women is no worse than our sin of resenting them for it.

So respond with grace to men who don't like you. Jesus did!

Respond with Patience

At Sue's former church, we prayed for many years for the male leaders to value our work. From the moment this request was on our lips, it tried our patience.

As the years passed without success, I once verbalized our prayer to a pastor. He responded, "Women's ministry is one of the best ministries in our church—if it ain't broke, don't fix it!" I wanted to shout, "It will break soon if things don't change!" I didn't. As I sent up a "flare" prayer, the Holy Spirit directed me to be quiet.

My concern for the welfare of the ministry was well founded. After four years of healthy, vibrant growth, the ministry faltered. Here's what happened.

Every two years, a new lay director led the ministry. Four years into the ministry, the job had grown so large no one wanted to serve. Besides, the director often clocked forty-hour weeks—sometimes even sixty! We couldn't find a lay leader called, equipped, and willing to put in those hours for no pay.

Our solution was to divide the job into three parts, giving an inexperienced woman the lead. She had the authority but little expertise. Everyone was frustrated. The original vision was sidetracked and the ministry suffered.

In addition, a catastrophic conflict erupted within women's ministries. The women's ministry leaders did not have the backing that staff members enjoyed. The conflict lasted over a year and crippled the ministry.

The leadership crisis and this conflict discouraged us all. With my joy waning and my zeal extinguished, I was tired. We had waited years and our patience had thinned—but we didn't dishonor God as we waited. And I'm grateful, because God was in the process of working.

Whatever your situation, wait on God. He sees and he knows. Give him time to work on your behalf. Remember: he is still a God of miracles!

Respond with Strength

Responding with grace and patience does not mean we are silent and weak. Vickie Kraft, former minister to women at Northwest Bible Church in Dallas for fourteen years, modeled Christlike courage when she worked on staff with men. She expected her church to pay her what a male pastor in a similar position earned. She asked for it graciously and they agreed.

During a staff meeting, one of the men argued that God exhibited only male attributes. Vickie countered with Bible verses where Paul described God in feminine terms. He resisted until finally Vickie suggested they talk later with another pastor present. Vickie never expressed anger or lost her composure. Neither did she back down.

Choose your battles carefully. Exhibit the fruit of the Spirit. Be a team player, not focused solely on your own agenda. Consider the cost. Don't nitpick. Study the previous section on conflict resolution and consult others before you proceed. But if God leads you to stand your ground, do so with dignity and backbone.

Respond with Excellence

[S]tand firm. Let nothing move you. *Always give yourselves fully to the work of the Lord,* because you know that your labor in the Lord is not in vain. (1 Cor. 15:58, emphasis added)

Strive for excellence in all you do. Don't focus on men who don't value you. Instead, focus on the Lord and the women he has called you to shepherd. He values you and he will sustain you. Don't obsess about the resources you lack. Be grateful for the resources God provides. Work hard and leave the results to him.

Respond with Faith

I (Sue) had served in a church where women's ministry wasn't valued; God then removed me and opened up two new opportunities—both on staff with pay and both serving with men who valued women. The two offers arrived within a month. For a woman who had ministered to women over twenty years and never attended a staff meeting or been paid a penny, it was "[a] good measure, pressed down, shaken together and running over" (Luke 6:38).

The first position was adviser to women students at Dallas Theological Seminary, where I trained in the 1980s. Though my role has since changed, I still love the stimulating academic atmosphere and working with women students.

I also served as pastor to women at Irving Bible Church, located in a suburb of Dallas. IBC is cutting-edge, Bible-based, and reaching out to both moderns and postmoderns. My time there resulted in years of productive, joyful ministry.

IBC employed four women pastors and eighteen women on support staff. I had four paid positions on my women's ministry staff—a director, an assistant director, and a fine arts coordinator in addition to myself.

I remember wondering if my days serving him were running out. I longed to be part of a team and enjoy the support of the leadership. Would God answer my prayer? I had no guarantees and neither do you. But God "acts on behalf of those who wait for him" (Isa. 64:4). Respond with faith, for he is your advocate. You never know what he is up to. I can testify that his plan is good! Have faith, stick around, and watch.

A Woman of Influence
DR. PAM MACRAE
by Natalie Edwards

As an advocate for women and educator of the Word of God, Pam MacRae trailblazes new paths for women at Moody Bible Institute and beyond. Pam's passion for ministering to the souls of women fueled parachurch work with women who have experienced exploitation. In addition, Pam speaks often at conferences and retreats designed for women. Her conference entitled Called: Equipping Women Who Lead to Make Disciples, which she began at Moody, was birthed out of a desire to train women called into ministry.

Pam's experience working with women in church and parachurch settings continues to inspire her work as professor at Moody Bible Institute, where God opened a new door in 2005. Pam finds joy in shaping future ministry leaders and teaches as professor in the Applied Theology and Church Ministry Division at Moody. There she serves as program head of two majors: Ministry to Women and Ministry to Victims of Sexual Exploitation.

With a DMin from Bethel Seminary in Congregational and Family Care with a Spiritual Formation emphasis, her role at Moody prepares both men and women to cultivate healthy methods in shepherding women in ministry. Having researched dynamics of male leadership in a mixed audience, her insight encourages meaningful conversation regarding gender roles in the church.

Embracing faith in Jesus at an early age, Pam discovered a desire to know God deeply. Her years learning from great Bible teachers while attending a Christian boarding school nurtured her love for God's Word and propelled her into further biblical training and fruitful ministry reaching women and men.

When away from the classroom, you'll find Pam relishing a good book, exploring the outdoors, and savoring time with family. Pam met her husband of thirty-eight years, Bob, at Moody Bible Institute. He serves as faculty at Moody Bible Institute as program head for the youth ministry major. Together, Pam and Bob have two daughters and six grandchildren.

PART 3

TAKING THE TRANSFORMATION MODEL TO THE CAMPUS

Chapter 14

WHO NEEDS A CAMPUS MINISTRY?

Every fall, women college students all over the nation sit in orientation, many feeling overwhelmed and facing tremendous adjustments. Many are still unpacking boxes in unfamiliar apartments with new roommates in a busy city far from home. Some have flown across oceans, others have relocated from across the country, and others simply came from across town.

Once the adviser to women students at DTS and now a professor, I (Sue) had the privilege of walking with women like these during their graduate studies. I met with each one for an entrance interview, and for those who needed it, I served as a sounding board, prayer partner, cheerleader, and mentor. Today I continue to meet those needs of women students as a professor, internship mentor, and friend.

MELISSA'S STORY

I noticed Melissa slip in late while I was welcoming the new women students at the orientation lunch. They sat around long tables decorated with red bandannas and Texas bluebonnets in cowboy boot vases, munching on tasty box lunches from a local deli. In four days they would walk into their first class at Dallas Theological Seminary.

Melissa grew up in a small Midwestern town and attended a state college a hundred miles from home. She came to faith through friends in her dorm who then nurtured her in their collegiate ministry on campus. As a result, she left behind her drinking buddies and focused on knowing her newfound love, Jesus. Although she graduated with honors, in her senior year she spent more time studying the Bible than the math textbooks required for her accounting degree. She was twenty-three years old and a baby believer—but God called her to serve him. So she flew across the country to study at DTS.

Ten days into the semester, she collapsed in my office weeping. Her mother had called the night before to inform her that she and her dad were divorcing. *The marriage has been a sham for years.* Melissa was stunned. Her world rocked, she came to unload and pray for God's direction. Should she continue her studies or go home? As we talked, other questions surfaced. So many fellow students it seemed to her had grown up in Christian homes and been to Bible college. Could she compete? She was thinking of changing her track from counseling to women's ministries or maybe even missions. What was *really* out there for women her age after graduation?

Melissa's life was at a critical juncture—just as mine had been when I was her age. I was not on a campus, but our needs were similar. We both needed an encourager who would show us how to rely on God in the midst of uncertainty and heartache. I found what I needed in a church's women's ministry. And she would be required to plug into a church during her Dallas stay. But due to time constraints and a different emphasis, she wasn't likely to become involved in the women's ministry in her church. She needed a ministry to women on campus. She found one, and a year later she was loving her studies, serving on the Women Students Fellowship Board, and processing her grief at her parents' split.

Do You See the Need on Your Campus?

Are you a student surrounded by women who need the support, encouragement, and inspiration that a ministry to women can provide? Maybe you are a professor or on staff and have observed this need for years. Or maybe you are a mother who wants these resources for your daughter and others who come behind her. You could be serving in a collegiate ministry that needs to get serious about meeting the needs of women students.

Can the Transformation Model be adapted to your campus setting? What would need to be changed? How would you get started? Who should lead a campus ministry? How will you maintain excellence and consistency when students are cycling in and out?

If you hear God's call to begin a campus ministry to women or you want to improve an existing one, read this section first. We will answer these and other related questions. We will supply resources and contacts to help you. After you've spent time digesting "how to's" specific to the campus, read part 2, *Taking the Transformation Model to the Church,* with the idea of adapting those principles to your campus.

WHEN GOD WENT AHEAD OF US

Let's begin with two remarkable examples of the way God planted campus ministries—first on a seminary campus and then on a secular campus.

Women's Ministry at DTS

Lisa Samra grew up on the DTS campus. Her dad was a professor and administrator, and her mom served on staff. After earning her undergraduate degree at the University of Texas, she returned to DTS, this time as a student. A gifted leader, Lisa saw the needs of women students and responded. When I was hired in 1998, God had already worked in Lisa's heart to begin the foundational preparation for the Women Students Fellowship Board. She would be the student leader in this new venture.

God linked Lisa, a postmodern woman, and myself, a modern woman, because he knew the ministry needed input and direction from us both. The campus had changed in the eight years since I had graduated. Besides, campus ministry is much more effective if it is student-led.

When I attended Dallas from 1985 to 1989, most women students, like myself, were experienced in ministry. DTS opened its doors to women in 1976 and by the late 1980s we made up about 12 percent of the student body. In contrast, today women account for about 40 percent of the student population, and many come right out of college with little ministry experience.

When I attended, DTS had the feel of a man's campus, and it was two years before I mustered the courage to ask a question in class. Please don't misunderstand. Women were welcomed and treated with respect. I was simply shy and in awe. Dallas turns out great Bible teachers and leaders and I felt honored to attend. But I allowed my timidity and reverence for the school to hinder my involvement. Although the campus had changed in many ways, many women students were still acting and feeling like I did as a student. God had done a great work in my life helping me overcome my apprehension and I wanted that for them. So did Lisa.

With Lisa as the first chairman, Women Students Fellowship Board launched during my first semester at DTS. God's timing is amazing. My work in academia and in the ministry trenches at IBC benefited both realms. And my twenty-five years' experience in women's ministry was a valuable resource to Lisa.

It's Made a Tremendous Difference!

When I met with incoming women students for a "get acquainted" interview, I asked them about their adjustment. The responses after our ministry was up and running differed greatly from those I heard when I first arrived, thanks to a ministry to women on campus.

"I feel right at home," answered Susan when I asked about her first semester. "I connected with several women at the orientation lunch and the brunch the next day. We went out over the weekend and when I walked into my first class, I already had friends."

Her comments are typical.

Wherever women gather, the potential for a women's ministry exists. On more and more campuses—both secular and Christian—women are adapting the Transformation Model.

Ministry to Women at Texas Tech University and Texas A&M

We always rented a trailer to take our children to college rather than my driving a second car. Why? Because I knew tears would hinder me driving back home. For both parents and their grown children, college is an enormous adjustment—and one often overlooked.

For Parents

For parents, the challenge involves knowing your offspring may never eat another vegetable. They can choose to stay out all night with people you will never meet. Will they find a church? Will it be your kind of church? Christian parents soon learn whether their son or daughter owns his or her faith.

For Students

College students make almost all their own decisions for the first time. Those who move far away from home must construct their social life all over again. They must navigate a new city and decipher a new campus. Vulnerable and sometimes naïve, freshmen especially risk making choices that sidetrack their progress and their faith. College years act as a vital bridge to adult life.

Sue's Story

Driving home after leaving my daughters, Heather and Rachel, at college was gut wrenching. At the time, I was studying 1 Peter and found comfort in the second chapter. Christ was alone, but he entrusted himself to God (1 Peter 2:23). All the way home I prayed silently, "Lord, I entrust them to you. Lord, I entrust them to you."

God answered my prayers through Patricia Hogan and Bonnie Turner. These young women were not students at my daughters' schools, but God gave them a vision to begin a ministry to women on their own campus, and it spread to other schools—including my daughters'.

They planted a Christian sorority at University of Texas in 1988 called Sigma Phi Lambda (Sisters for the Lord) and chapters had spread to Texas Tech and Texas A&M by the time my daughters enrolled.

It Made a Tremendous Difference There, Too

Through "Phi Lamb," Christian women develop meaningful friendships, pray, and study the Bible together, and best of all, the organization is open to anyone. Their vision made an enormous difference in my daughters' lives and answered the prayers of a mother Patricia and Bonnie never met.

My daughter Heather writes:

> Phi Lamb was probably one of the greatest positive spiritual influences during my college years. The accountability, fellowship, and lifelong friendships created between us were essential to my growth in Christ. The small prayer groups and prayer partners encouraged me. I learned to be vulnerable and honest with fellow sisters who lifted up my needs to the Lord.
>
> Having friends to hang out with that were positive spiritual influences helped provide alternatives to the typical negative

peer pressure faced by college students. I had many opportunities to serve Christ through leading small groups, playing my guitar for worship, and mentoring younger sisters. I've been gone over twenty years, but I still keep in contact with many of my Phi Lamb sisters. I thank God for this incredible gift of true friendships that continue to spur me on in my relationship with God. (So does her mom!)

How would you plant a campus women's ministry with this kind of impact? Read on.

A Woman of Influence
DR. KAREN SWALLOW PRIOR
by Lindsay Ann Nickens

"My passion for life and learning and human flourishing begins and ends with Christ," says Karen Swallow Prior, English professor at Liberty University, a private Christian university in Lynchburg, Virginia. Teaching is only one outlet of many that manifests her love for "life, learning, and God."

Karen earned her credentials at secular universities, her BA at Daemen College in Amherst, New York, and her MA and PhD at the State University of New York at Buffalo. She credits both her secular education and her previous career as a teacher and principal of a Christian high school as preparation for her fundamental understanding of the synthesis between education and Christianity. She states, "Christian education requires students to learn what is taught in secular schools and then to do the additional work of critiquing and discerning that material using the Bible and theology as a measure. This experience primed me for the teaching I now do at the university level."[35]

Karen's tenacity for wider education that coincides with a biblical worldview extends beyond the classroom. She contributes articles to secular and religious magazines and has authored several books. She is a researcher for the Ethics and Religious Liberty Commission, works on the Board of Trustees of Faith and Action, and is a Senior Research Fellow at The Trinity Forum. Culture and Christianity dialogue in much of Karen's work as she informs her audience in a wide variety of topics. Karen's books include *On Reading Well: Finding the Good Life through Great Books*, *Fierce Convictions: The Extraordinary Life of Hannah More: Poet, Reformer, Abolitionist*, and *Booked: Literature in the Soul of Me*.[36]

Karen's passion for life, however, expands beyond academia. An ardent animal lover with a fervor for God's creation, Karen lives on nine acres of property with various animals, including chickens, dogs, and horses. Also living among these creatures are Karen's husband, Roy, and her parents, who reside in a house Roy built for them on the property.

Chapter 15

CREATE YOUR OWN
CAMPUS WOMEN'S MINISTRY

How will you begin? Here's a plan that works on both Christian and secular campuses.

Evaluate Your Campus Atmosphere

What Are Their Ages and Stages?

Who are the women on your campus? Is this their first time away from home, or have they had several years to adjust to living on their own at other schools? Are you at an undergraduate or graduate school? A ministry to women at a medical school will look different than one at a community college.

What are their ages? Are they mostly the same age—or do women from different ages and stages attend your school?

Are They Single or Married?

The social needs of single women differ from those of married women. Singles sometimes have more time to participate in a campus ministry and are more likely to volunteer to help. If you plan a Saturday night outing, don't expect many married women to attend. Older married women may have established themselves in a profession, or they may have family responsibilities that limit their time. Find out who needs your ministry and mold it with them in mind.

Do many married men attend your school? If so, do you want to include their wives in your ministry? At DTS we realize that wives will be partnering with their husbands in the pastorate, mission field, and other ministries.

Even though these women are not attending seminary, their training is often crucial to their husbands' success. A women's ministry can prepare these wives.

However, at DTS the needs of student wives and women students are radically different. Student wives need Bible training and mentoring, but women seminary students already receive this training in their courses. Long before Lisa dreamed of a ministry for women students, DTS faculty wives had organized to train the wives.

Therefore, DTS has two women's ministries—one for wives and one for women students. Some women fit both descriptions and can partake of either fare. Occasionally they partner to bring in a speaker both groups enjoy or on a project for the school. But otherwise these groups are designed to meet the unique needs of each group. In a secular school, ask the question, "Do wives and women students share the same needs?" If they do, structure a ministry to both. If they don't, keep them separate.

Where Do They Live?

Do most of the women live in the dorms or at home? Are you at a commuter school? Dorm life automatically brings women together socially. Usually activities are already planned and people are readily available for support and fun. It's hard to be lonely in the dorm.

But women on a commuter campus are more likely to come and go quickly. DTS is located downtown and housing is in short supply. Many women live in apartments throughout the city and local residents drive long distances to class. Even though many want to connect, it's a challenge.

At a commuter school you will need to offer activities and ministries when the majority of women are on campus.

Where Are They From?

Are women students mainly local, or have they come from around the nation or the world? If your campus is in a large city, women from small towns are often overwhelmed initially as they learn to navigate the traffic and find their way around. If they come from other countries, they may experience language and cultural barriers. Women who travel far to attend your school probably won't know anyone when they arrive.

What is the racial mix? Do your women tend to segregate by race or are they comfortable with one another? How will your women's ministry bring women with different perspectives together for the benefit of all?

We draw women from all over the nation and the world. Many arrive alone and overwhelmed. They believe God has called them to a life of service but are uncertain where to find the needed resources. The first few weeks are critical to a healthy adjustment, true on most campuses. How will you help them connect and settle in? We'll show you.

DTS intentionally mixes women of different races and nationalities together from their first day on campus. Often barriers never arise because the women feel loved and cared for as individuals and they have shared newcomer experiences.

Also, DTS intentionally recruits board leaders from different races and nationalities. As the board prays and plans together, women present different perspectives that might be overlooked if the leadership didn't reflect a mix.

If you draw women from a variety of places and backgrounds, consider it a blessing and communicate that attitude to your women. Instead of causing conflict or divisiveness, variety is a plus that can enrich the lives of women and model true Christlike love on the campus.

Are You at a Christian or Secular Campus?

If secular, Christian women yearn to find one another and form a community where they can grow spiritually and encourage each other in their faith. Usually their values and standards are different from the college culture, and they appreciate a haven where they are accepted and strengthened to be salt and light on campus. A ministry to women can transform a Christian woman's experience at a secular college.

Sigma Phi Lambda provides a successful model of a Christian organization on a secular campus. That model will look different if you are planting a ministry to women at a Bible college, seminary, or school supported by a particular denomination. If Bible studies are common or students are required to take Bible courses, your structure may not need to include Bible study. At DTS the greatest need is for community and connection among women. The DTS ministry takes on an entirely different flavor from Sigma Phi Lambda.

Study the demographics of your women before you begin. Until you know who they are, you won't know how to structure a ministry to meet their needs. Is the need spiritual, social, or academic? Where should you focus first? What's already in place? You don't want to duplicate what others are doing. After you assess the needs on campus, consider who will lead the ministry.

WHO SHOULD LEAD A CAMPUS WOMEN'S MINISTRY?

Is God showing *you* the needs on your campus? Do you have a passion to change the environment for women? Great! God put these desires within you for a reason. But are you a student, or a staff or faculty member? Your status determines how you should proceed.

Will your ministry be to students? If so and you are on staff or a professor, ask God to show you a student with the same vision and heart. Students will understand the campus from a unique perspective that staff and faculty cannot share. Other students will be more likely to join in if they are led by one of their own. A student organization is better student-bred and -led.

If you are a student, ask God to identify a woman staff member or professor to assist you. You may need a long-term advocate on campus or a woman with more experience to help you through conflict or crises. If you need financial assistance from your school, she may be instrumental in securing the budget you need to function. She may serve as the liaison between you and the administration, helping you to understand the system and accomplish tasks more quickly.

When the DTS women's board chairman had to make a choice between serving on the board or working to pay her tuition, I was able to bless her with a scholarship. When women want to use their board service hours for an internship, that faculty liaison can serve as their required supervisor. Certainly the staff or faculty member should not micromanage the organization. But partnering with her will benefit everyone.

DETERMINE YOUR MINISTRY STRUCTURE

How Will You Begin?

- Gather a team of interested women to pray, brainstorm, and plan.

- Write a vision, mission, and/or purpose statement to help maintain perspective.

For example, the DTS organization now known as Arise Women Student Fellowship (ARISE) says it exists "to foster community among DTS women for the purpose of honoring our God-given worth, maintaining high academic standards, building friendships and abiding fellowship, and developing ministry opportunities."

MISSION STATEMENT

ARISE endeavors to glorify God as we connect, engage, and encourage the community of women students at Dallas Theological Seminary by:

- *cultivating unity* within the body of women—and within the whole student body, the Seminary, and the body of Christ—through open dialogue on relevant issues and providing leadership and serving opportunities for women students, and
- *celebrating diversity* through the promotion of authentic relationships as we equip, prepare, and launch into our callings.

Their theme verse is Isaiah 60:1, "Arise, shine, for your light has come, and the glory of the Lord rises upon you."

For more information visit their website www.dts.edu/arise. You can learn more from their constitution in Appendix E.

Sigma Phi Lambda states its vision and purpose on its website, www.sigmaphilambda.org:

Sigma Phi Lambda (ΣΦΛ) is a Christian sorority that strives to glorify God by providing a source of fellowship for college women who sincerely seek to know His person, His will, and His ways. It is a non-denominational organization of sisters where fellowship with our most high God is fostered by growth in unity with one another. Through weekly meetings that include worship, encouragement, fellowship, and accountability, Phi Lamb provides an alternative to Panhellenic sororities. Sigma Phi Lambda is not presently, nor will it ever be Panhellenic.

Their theme verse is Romans 15:5–6, "May the God who gives endurance and encouragement give you the same attitude of mind toward each other that Christ Jesus had, so that with one mind and one voice you may glorify the God and Father of our Lord Jesus Christ."

Sigma Phi Lambda exists for the sole purpose of glorifying our Lord Jesus Christ and making his name great.

Learn how to begin a chapter and more on their website, www.sigmaphil-ambda.org.

As you structure your lead team or board and ministries, ask, "Does it line up with our vision, mission, or purpose statement?" If not, you risk sidetracking the ministry.

WRITE YOUR CONSTITUTION

Becoming a student organization is often a lengthy process. You will probably need to apply for a charter. At some schools you are also required to apply for tax-exempt status and recruit a faculty adviser. To begin the process, write your constitution. This document describes the way your organization will function. It contains sections entitled Name, Purpose, Membership, Officers, Structure, Meetings, Methods to Amend the Constitution, Bylaws, and any other information particular to your organization.

How do you know what officers you'll need on your team? Again, look at your vision or purpose statement. What are the greatest needs? Why do you exist? What will your calendar look like? What ministries will you create to meet those needs? You'll need leaders to lead these ministries.

DETERMINE YOUR MINISTRIES

Here are some ideas that might help you get started.

Dallas Theological Seminary

Orientation Ministry

The first few months on campus often determine whether a student thrives or fails. How can you help students acclimate quickly?

At DTS, before women arrived on campus, they received an invitation to our welcome luncheon. They also had the option of joining a fellowship group led by a returning student. The first year we offered these groups, 90 percent of the women participated.

We held our lunch at a time women were already on campus for orientation—so that we reach them before classes began. We decorated the room, served a delicious lunch, and played games that forced them to get out of their chairs and interact. Living the same experience bonded them quickly.

During lunch, the board chair and I welcomed the women and explained what to expect. Returning students acted out skits and used other creative methods to help the new students laugh and relax. After lunch they met with their fellowship group and received a map and an invitation to brunch the next day. Informal brunches were held in homes and apartments on Saturday morning, but the women often stayed into the afternoon. At these brunches, relationships were birthed.

The fellowship groups continued to meet monthly during the fall, but often women formed their own organic communities after the brunch. Whether or not a new student attended all these gatherings, she still had a friend and resource in her fellowship group leader. Getting off to a good start made a tremendous difference.

Retreat

Nothing bonds women like a block of time away. What kind of retreat would work for your campus? Can you get away to a retreat center, a local hotel, or even a facility on the campus overnight?

We carpooled to a country retreat center about an hour out of Dallas— quiet and green, with enough rocking chairs on a porch by the lake to accommodate almost everyone. We held this retreat early in the semester before "crunch" time, and we only stayed Friday night through Saturday afternoon to suit homework demands. Although the retreat devoured a sizable chunk of our yearly budget, it was worth it.

To learn how to organize and implement a retreat, read chapter 10, Offer Exciting Events. Adjust to your budget and time frame.

Brown Bags and Seminars

What topics of particular interest to women are not addressed in their courses? Identify women speakers from among your faculty and community that women students would benefit from hearing. What women's issues need to be highlighted on campus? Be sure to build in lots of student participation time at these events.

At DTS, women students expressed their interests by showing up to learn and discuss topics like women and pornography, ministering to women with same-sex attraction, women caught in domestic violence, surviving conflict in ministry . . . just a small sampling of issues they will face in ministry. Our enrichment coordinators planned a smörgåsbord of gatherings that focused on women's needs and issues.

Graduating Women's Luncheon

What kinds of celebrations warrant a party you can host? What will women remember about their college days that will last a lifetime and affect their future involvement with the school? A strong ministry to women often takes the initiative to make memories.

We treated our women graduates to a sumptuous luncheon complete with crystal vases and fresh flowers. I purchased the vases on sale and used them year after year. I gave each graduate a print of Jesus holding a lamb to remind them of who they are and what he is sending them out to do. You'll find this print framed in offices and homes all over the country and the world—a symbol that bonds us together. We recruited alumnae to speak and encourage the women as they set out to serve. We photographed the class and sent out complimentary copies. What kinds of memories can you make on your campus?

How Often Should You Meet to Implement Your Ministries?

We learned to focus on key needs and not to do too much. Women students are busy with assignments, work, or family responsibilities. We were careful not to overload our calendar with activities during midterms and finals—and not to burden our leaders with unnecessary meetings.

The DTS board met monthly during the fall and spring semesters for about an hour and a half, during the day that was convenient for everyone. We traveled to a bed and breakfast for a spring training camp to transition between the old and new board and to prepare for the year ahead. Also, we asked the board to support one another's activities. Most women students can't commit to much more.

We've provided a sampling of ministries at DTS. What works on a secular campus? Let's look at the ministries of Phi Lamb and how they originated.

Sigma Phi Lambda (Sisters for the Lord) at University of Texas

Junior Tricia Adams dreamed of a sorority that was not exclusive like the Panhellenic organizations. Its motto would be, "You choose us. We don't choose you." She dreamed of a Christian community on her campus composed of women from different denominations yet united in Christian love and purpose, an organization that propelled women deeper into an intimate relationship with Jesus through prayer, Bible study, and mentoring.

In 1988, Tricia gathered a team of like-minded women and founded Sigma Phi Lambda on the University of Texas campus. They began with five founders and eight charter members. During the fall they tried out their ideas and formulated them into a constitution. They joined the UT rush for the first time in the spring and netted nine pledges—almost doubling their membership.

As of summer 2018 her dream has taken root at thirty-one other colleges where women students have established new chapters. Phi Lamb has grown to impact thousands of women. How did they structure their ministry? What ministries are in place to serve their members? How similar are the original organization and its sister chapters?

Phi Lamb's Ministries

Phi Lamb requires its members to attend a local church, be involved in a Bible study of their choice, meet with a Phi Lamb prayer group once a week, and attend 80 percent of their meetings and a retreat each semester. They also join together in community service projects.

"Through Phi Lamb, Jesus has become more real. It has influenced every aspect of my college life—especially my prayer life. It's where I found my friends," says Mandi Waldrip, a former Texas Tech Phi Lamb president.

Members meet regularly to sing, pray, share, conduct business, and hear an inspirational speaker.

"Phi Lamb is a great evangelistic tool. Our pledges are mature Christians, new believers, and even some seekers. The officers meet with every new woman to assess needs and have the opportunity to present the gospel," says Mandi.

If you choose to partner with Phi Lamb, they will help you get started. "What is so amazing is to see the same spirit in each chapter. We ensure consistency and purpose by asking each chapter to follow the same constitution," says Bonnie Collins Turner, former board member.

What is this successful college ministry doing that inspires you? How will you structure your ministry and implement the ministries for the women on your campus? Once you have made these decisions, you need women to lead.

CHOOSE YOUR LEADERSHIP TEAM MEMBERS

Every organization needs a leader. The DTS ARISE board chairperson is a student chosen from the existing board by the current board chairperson and the adviser to women students. She serves for a year. Other board positions include vice president, secretary, treasurer, chaplain, publicity chair, retreat co-chairs, communications chair, hospitality chair, and connections chair.

Each Phi Lamb chapter elects its own officers, and they receive support and guidance from an alumnae council, made up of alumnae who served as officers in that chapter, and a regional director, who is also a Phi Lamb alumna. Each chapter selects a president, vice president, chaplain, treasurer, and secretary. Every group will take on a different flavor. Choose your leadership positions to fit your needs.

WORK WITH THE ADMINISTRATION

Stay on Track

To be most effective, ministry needs consistency in purpose and vision. On a campus, many students are cycling in and out every four years. Who is around for the long haul? Who passes on hard-learned lessons and ensures the team doesn't get sidetracked? Often the faculty adviser, women's director, or dean of women works closely with the student-led ministry and can be the consistent thread needed. Include her graciously and seek her counsel.

If your school does not provide a woman leader for students, identify a woman working in administration, student services, or dean's office and ask her to be the liaison between your group and the rest of the administration.

If you are a student, what is your attitude toward the faculty and staff? Do you resent their involvement? Are you willing to learn from their experience? Certainly, the adviser should not run the ministry, oversee meetings, or be involved in the details. But her expertise, experience, and understanding of how to work with the administration can be an asset to your organization.

Be Flexible and Cooperative!

Who keeps the calendar at your school? Be sure you check the school's calendar before you schedule activities or events. Be known as a flexible organization taking other group's plans into account and not insisting on your own way.

Every school operates differently. If it is a private or religious institution, it must consider the opinions of supporters and donors in its policies and decisions. You may not always understand the reasons behind restrictions placed on student organizations, but you will honor God and earn a good name for your group by cooperating with the administration and abiding by its guidelines.

Resolve Conflict Together

Conflict is inevitable in any ministry. Your adviser probably has experience resolving conflict and should be alerted if parties clash. One year a conflict arose at DTS between two student organizations. The board president tried to handle it on her own but only made it worse. By the time I learned of the conflict, several women were wounded and angry.

The board president asked me to intervene after the damage. When we sat down to talk I suggested that if she had come to me earlier, we could have averted hurt feelings and ill will between the two organizations. She agreed. Then we prayed together and brainstormed how to deal with the dispute. We gathered all the involved parties, apologized, and talked out our differences. Take advantage of your adviser's expertise.

PROVIDE ROLE MODELS AND MENTORS

Many women earn undergraduate and graduate degrees while in their twenties. Of course, older women also pursue degrees. What's the attitude of younger women students toward older women professors, staff, and students? Most younger students yearn to connect with older women for mentoring and discipleship. But like in a church, most older women won't volunteer their expertise and wisdom. You must ask. For more insight on how to facilitate healthy mentoring relationships between generations, read Sue's book *Organic Mentoring*.

DTS offers a four-year Master of Theology and many two-year Master of Arts degrees. ARISE draws on the women faculty and administrators to share their expertise. Ask influential women on your campus to speak at your seminars, brown bags, and retreats. Many are right under your nose—treasures who have a heart for students. Don't overlook them.

HOW WILL YOU CREATE YOUR OWN CAMPUS WOMEN'S MINISTRY?

In a nutshell . . .

- Evaluate your campus atmosphere.
- Decide who should be the key leader of the ministry.
- Determine your ministry structure.
- Choose the officers to lead those ministries.
- Work with the administration.
- Provide role models and mentors.

Women on campuses everywhere are hungry for the relationships, encouragement, and inspiration that a ministry to women provides. Is God calling you to be his initiator? If so, step out and go for it! Women's lives can be transformed through a women's ministry on the campus just like in the church or on the mission field.

A Woman of Influence
DR. SANDRA GLAHN
by Kelley Mathews

"My current ministry was birthed from an identity crisis," Dr. Sandra Glahn, Associate Professor of Media Arts and Worship at Dallas Theological Seminary, often tells those who inquire about her career as an author and seminary professor. A native of Oregon, Sandra began her affiliation with DTS when her husband, Gary, studied there in the 1980s. Having earlier earned her BA at Washington Bible College, she pursued a career in communications while he studied.

As time went on, they began a ten-year struggle with infertility that carried over into pregnancy loss and failed adoptions. Thus began the self-described identity crisis: if motherhood was the pinnacle of Christian womanhood, as was commonly taught in the church, where did that leave her and other women dealing with infertility?

Toward the end of that season, Sandra—by now a seminary student herself—partnered with her seminary-trained obstetrician to write the book *When Empty Arms Become a Heavy Burden*. In it, they addressed infertility from the personal, spiritual, and medical perspectives. This led to a season of writing and speaking about bioethics, sexuality, and reproductive technologies. Not content just to instruct readers, the duo also teamed up to write several medical suspense novels, including the CBA bestseller and Christy Award finalist *Lethal Harvest*.

While at DTS, Glahn mentored other writers and assisted the school's media arts department. By the time she graduated with her Master of Theology degree, she was teaching writing courses at DTS and serving her church as director of women's ministry. There, Glahn wrote her own Bible studies for women. Those inductive studies became the foundation for a new line of published works, the Coffee Cup Bible study series, which currently includes eleven titles.

As she pursued PhD studies at the University of Texas at Dallas, Glahn joined the faculty of DTS as associate professor and editor-in-chief of the seminary's magazine, *Kindred Spirit* (now *DTS Magazine*), which won numerous awards during her tenure. Teaching courses in writing and on gender in the church, she finds students—women in particular—struggling with the same fear of being "less than" that she faced decades earlier. She repeatedly affirms to her students that a woman's greatest calling is not to support a husband or mother children, but to image God and exercise dominion over the earth.

Most recently Glahn demonstrated her own theological expertise by pulling together and editing *Vindicating the Vixens*, which examines unfairly maligned or ignored women in the Bible. Championing accurate historical and cultural analysis that clarifies what biblical authors were trying to communicate, Glahn continues to challenge her students toward thinking that transforms.

She and Gary, a missionary with East-West Ministries, live in Texas with their daughter, Alexandra.

PART 4

CONVERTING THE TRANSFORMATION MODEL CROSS-CULTURALLY

CHAPTER 16

STRATEGIES THAT WORK WORLDWIDE

Many churches in my country are led by women who have no training. Will you take a team to train them in the spring?" Celestin's eyes danced as he spoke about his native land, Rwanda, in Central Africa. They darkened as he described the 1994 genocide massacre, when over eight hundred thousand of his people were murdered by warring tribes—among them five family members.

Celestin conveyed the situation: With the deaths of so many men, women stepped up as pastors rather than leave their churches leaderless. But most were discouraged. The needs were overwhelming. They had few resources—many didn't even own a Bible. Celestin informed us that there had never been a women's ministry conference in Rwanda. He wanted to sponsor the first—and he wanted me to lead it.

"I'll pray about it," I responded, butterflies already fluttering inside. *Where is Rwanda? Why does he want me?* I had traveled extensively growing up, but I had little experience on the mission field.

Celestin Musakura's six-foot frame towered over the American women he had invited to lunch. His ink-black skin and bright orange African flowered shirt turned heads as we paraded into Bruno's Italian Restaurant. While he was completing his doctorate at Dallas Seminary, he organized and often led training in Africa five or six times a year. His ministry, ALARM—African Leadership and Reconciliation Ministry—still trains male pastors, but now his passion has extended to equipping women leaders and pastors' wives.

Five months after lunch at Bruno's, our team of five, including Celestin's wife Bernadette, hopscotched across three continents en route to Kigali,

Rwanda's capital, where we trained eighty-four women leaders from all over the tiny nation.

Can you counsel grieving women or teach the Bible? What have you learned from walking with the Lord that could encourage women in other countries? I never imagined God would call me to Africa, but he did. He might call you too.

ADAPT THE TRANSFORMATION MODEL

Women on every continent want to minister to one another. Women minister to one another naturally but, just like with the Rwandan women, they hear what's happening in America and they want it too. The Transformation Model is cross-cultural. Of course, it must be adapted in other countries to fit their needs and methods—but the heart of it is transferable. Women everywhere want an intimate relationship with Jesus, to know the Bible, and to connect and serve.

For this chapter, we interviewed experienced women missionaries who shared principles and projects that transform lives in other cultures. Take what you have learned in parts 1 and 2 and adapt it to your own missions setting.

THINK OUTSIDE THE BOX

Since biblical times, women have obeyed the Great Commission by planting churches, preaching, teaching, and healing across the world—sometimes alone. Examples include New Testament women Priscilla and Lydia as well as more contemporary models like Amy Carmichael (born 1867), Mary Slessor (born 1848), and Lottie Moon (born 1846). Their noble work continues, but now new doors are opening for women in cross-cultural women's ministries—both short- and long-term.

Do you love women where you are but also hear God's call beyond your borders or out into diverse communities? Is your primary calling at home but you also hear a secondary call to missions? Is it possible to do both? Does a global heart beat within you but circumstances hinder you from living overseas?

Today a missionary doesn't necessarily need to uproot permanently. Missions in a postmodern world looks different. New methods and strategies give women unheard of opportunities to minister cross-culturally. The wide availability of the internet helps us connect anywhere in the world in an instant. With faster travel, we can target a group and return intermittently to build and equip them—for the purpose of growing them so that one day they won't need us. In the twenty-first century, missions has a new face.

I (Sue) dismissed missions—in fact, the idea scared me—but God opened short-term doors that broadened my perspective and enriched my ministry at home. His plan for you may include surprises—short-term projects, living in another land, or maybe even in another part of your city. Does your pulse race as you read these words? If so, God could be calling you to missions. How will you know? Ask God for direction and learn all you can.

Cross-cultural ministry is more than packing your bags and setting out with good intentions. Women who impact others across the globe are savvy. They proceed with a plan. And they network with others.

What would you need to know to oversee a missions ministry in a church? How do women today prepare themselves for high impact, short-term trips? How do you know when God is calling you to uproot for a long-term commitment? In this section, we'll explore key components to cross-cultural ministry.

DETERMINE YOUR SCOPE

"For a long time, missionaries could go anywhere in the world and do almost anything with the assurance that it would be useful and productive. But we can no longer go anywhere without risking overlap or interference with the legitimate work of others. We are part of a global missions movement and we must find our most valuable and productive roles," says missions strategist David Mays.[37]

What if God calls you to minister in a church to diverse women across your city or across the globe? Strategic ministers must focus their efforts and determine their scope. How can you ensure that your ministry is strategically driven?

CREATE YOUR STRATEGY

Whether you belong to a small church, a large church, or a parachurch organization, strategy is critical. Examine this example and apply their experience to your own setting.

A Parachurch Strategy for Russia

At least 80 percent of Russian church members are female. Yet training for ministry to women was almost nonexistent prior to the 1990s. However, in 1992, three Russian women spread a map of their native Russia across a table, stretched their arms over it, and prayed. Teardrops spotted the vast expanse. Their request? Lord, send us training so we can minister to women in our churches.

Was their request too big for God? No, but the answer was almost a decade in the making. A national women's ministry training project, "Christian Women in Partnership—Russia," was birthed in 1999. God networked key Russian and American leaders and a variety of parachurch mission organizations to fashion an in-depth, long-term training program for gifted Russian women leaders. The goal was to reach and transform thousands of Russian women all over Russia's eleven time zones. The result? The project trained—and continues to train—thousands of women across the entire country. How did God orchestrate this amazing story?

God crafted a beautiful mosaic etched at different times in different places all over the world to answer their prayer. "We felt like we were skiing behind a 747," says Gail Seidel, a key American player.

Puzzle Piece #1: God Prepared the Curriculum

At the same time the three Russian women prayed, American missionary Wendy Wilson was developing a seven-course curriculum for women in Eastern Europe. She worked with Biblical Education by Extension International (BEE). The courses were translated into Romanian, Bulgarian, Czech, Hungarian, and Polish. They also translated the courses into Russian even though there was no existing place to use the material at that time.

Puzzle Piece #2: God Prepared Three Women in the East

Valentina

In 1992, Valentina Karchazhkina, a former Communist Party leader and proponent of Marxist philosophy, heard John Maisel speak at Moscow State University. John was the president of East-West Ministries International

(EWMI). Valentina gave her life to Christ and grew quickly in her faith. A former linguistics professor and fluent in English, she was hired in EWMI's Moscow office to minister to women.

Vera

In 1998, Vera Kadaeva heard John speak at a Russian women's conference. The daughter of a Baptist pastor, Vera was persecuted for her faith even before she became a Christian and, after accepting the Lord during her college years, spent time in a mental hospital as the government tried to reindoctrinate her to atheistic communism.

Liz

American Liz Loeffler had served as a missionary for Greater Europe Missions (GEM) since 1993 and began ministering in Moscow a year later. She was on loan to BEE in their Women's Ministries Department and then in 1998 to EWMI, where she assisted Valentina. The two Russians, Valentina and Vera, and American Liz shared a vision to train Russian women and began meeting in Moscow to consider the possibilities.

Puzzle Piece #3: God Prepared Women in the West

In 1998, in Dallas, John Maisel initiated a meeting with Gail Seidel, a missionary on furlough with BEE, and Gwynne Johnson, a BEE board member. John expressed his desire to see a nationwide women's ministry training program birthed. Within an hour, all three agreed to invite their Russian colleagues to a strategy meeting in Dallas to explore what God might do as they pooled their resources. However, the meeting was delayed due to scheduling problems.

Puzzle Piece #4: God Prepared an Indispensable Russian Man

During this delay, God enlisted another key player. Peter Konovaltchik was the head of the Union of Evangelical Christians-Baptists of Russia (UECB). This umbrella organization includes the majority of evangelical churches in Russia, and Peter wielded tremendous influence over them. As he saw the vast need for women's ministry, he blessed the idea of a national women's ministry training program. He was instrumental in promoting the ministry within individual churches throughout Russia. Without his endorsement, the vision that God was working out in John and these key women in both the East and the West would never have materialized.

Puzzle Piece #5: God Prepared Additional Women

In January 1999, Russian and American women met for two days at a Dallas home to hammer out a comprehensive strategy. Valentina, Vera, Liz, Wendy, Gail, and Gwynne were there along with others who would later serve as faculty, on a Dallas board, or on a national board of reference.

Simultaneously, on the other side of the world, God was preparing the hearts of twenty-one Russian women leaders throughout the eleven time zones to respond to an invitation to participate in that strategy. Their decision would not only transform their lives but those of thousands of their sisters.

Here was the strategy:

- Five regions were identified across Russia.
- Three Russian women leaders were selected from each region by the Russian Baptist superintendents. (Several others were later invited, making the number of students twenty-one.)
- Twenty-one students traveled to Moscow three times a year for training in the seven-course curriculum. (The courses were Discovery Bible Study and teacher training, a women's ministry "how to" class, Spiritual Life, Evangelism and Discipleship, Marriage, Family, and "Developing a Discerning Heart" counselor training.)
- The instruction lasted for six years. Students made a long-term commitment to intensive training.
- Classes were taught by a Western faculty. The students read books and completed weighty assignments between classes.
- In groups of three, the students established regional women's ministry training centers.
- The goal was to birth additional local training centers and ultimately smaller training centers in individual churches. The

goal was for this strategy to potentially equip over 2,300 Russian women leaders.

Here's What God Did!

Leaders of the National Women's Ministries Training Program in Russia sent us their most recent report (2018) that showcases eighteen years of fruitful ministry. Highlights include:

- The project continues to impact the vast Russian nation with multiplication to the fourth generation.
- Russian nationals are equipped, leading, and owning the ministry.
- The project is self-sustaining and firmly established at the local church level.
- Responsibility for funding has passed effectively to Russian churches and other national resources.
- Countless women are studying the Bible for the first time due to the requirement that each student start a small group study during their first year in the program.
- Russian pastors testify that their churches are stronger and the women are united and mobilizing others to study the Bible, to ministry, and to outreach as well as building into their families.
- Many Russian pastors and churches are embracing the value of training women for ministry.

Summary statistics:

- Nine hundred eighty-seven women completed the training and graduated from eighty-six training centers between September 1999 and July 2018.
- Four levels of multiplication (one Base Training Center, seven Regional Training Centers, twenty-two Local Training Centers, and seventy-seven City Training Centers thus far)
- Twenty-one City Training Centers still training 310 women
- Four new City Training Centers in process of starting

What the Training Meant to Russian Students

- *I've waited twenty-one years for training like this.*
- *You have taught us how to smile.*
- *I had no idea that I'd ever teach the Bible. God made me adequate for that.*
- *I hope my students will love me as much as we love you.*

What the Training Meant to Ministry Leaders

Vera Kadaeva, one of the three key Russian leaders, reflected,

> It was really from the Lord, from above, because he has a dream about this, and he shared this dream with our American sisters and with us. And he provided everything. So, it's very good to be in his dream! Because it's true that we limit him—we limit him by our human limitations. I remember when this training opened and John Maisel, in his speech, challenged us to believe, to live by grace. And he said, "To believe is not easy. You need to sit on the edge of the boat, put your foot in the water, and then walk! It's not easy."

Mary Dean, Former Director of Women's Ministries, Stonebriar Community Church (Frisco, Texas), recalled:

> I never imagined that I would be traveling to Moscow on a regular basis to be part of a teaching team for a project of this size. What a privilege it has been to connect with women from a different country. We speak different languages, face different challenges, live in completely different worlds, and yet, we love the same Lord, have the same dreams for our families, share many struggles, and have grown to love one another.

And Joye Baker, Adjunct Professor and Women's Adviser, Dallas Theological Seminary, remarked:

When we first met the Russian women, they lacked confidence. Our training and personal interaction with them has helped them to grow in their understanding and abilities to equip their Russian sisters. They are now enthusiastically spreading the love and hope of Jesus Christ across their vast country. And their faith in God and commitment to women's ministry training has been an inspiration to me personally.

WHY IS THIS STRATEGY WORKING?

Notice that this ministry is not territorial. They combined vision and resources and didn't care who received credit. Also, the Americans and Russians shared leadership. Both overcame language and cultural barriers to work together toward a common dream. Americans were willing to be led by Russian women with less training and fewer resources because the Russian women better understood what worked in their own country. Strong leaders humble themselves and submit to others' ideas for the greater good.

As a result, God answered the tearful prayers of three Russian women who prayed over a map. How? He sculpted the lives of called men and women. He placed them in crucial places at particular times. He orchestrated their days so that they crossed paths and came together to carry out his plans—ordinary people just like you and me who were willing to listen to God and follow him. God can use you to impact your world for Jesus too.

One caveat to consider, however, comes from missionary Kaley Harper:

> The Russian strategy works very well in literate cultures, but in areas of deep poverty the vast majority of the church is female and, significantly, illiterate. Therefore training looks different. If a teacher is engaging in those cultures, I would encourage them to continue to be creative, listen, and adapt to the needs of the people. It was very humbling the first time I taught a group that couldn't read my notes, who had a third-grade education but no Bibles, yet who desperately wanted to know about God. As long as we are being creative Spirit-led teachers, God will continue to work powerfully in their lives and hearts.

But can it happen without a strategy? Not a chance.

WHAT ARE THE ADVANTAGES OF A STRATEGY?

By using a bullet rather than buckshot approach, you are a good steward of the money and people God entrusts to you. A hit-or-miss plan is difficult to evaluate, but with a narrow focus, evaluation is easier—and so is impact! When you determine your scope you are far less likely to become sidetracked.

You research the target areas—you don't have to be an expert on every place in the world. But you become an expert on some.

You can connect multiple short-term trips into long-term projects. If the goal is training leaders, train them in stages. If evangelism, follow up when another team returns. If discipleship, a return trip provides accountability. Whatever the ministry, a return trip increases productivity. With a strategy you are assured of a visible, significant impact.

People on your teams invest in long-term relationships. On the first few trips you earn trust and credibility. Follow-up trips are more productive when solid relationships between the team and nationals already exist.

Put in the time up front to plan and prepare carefully. Depend on God every step. Don't be afraid of big plans because he is a big God. Remember: it won't happen without strategic planning, prayer, and a limited scope.

A Woman of Influence
KALEY HARPER
by Amanda Sherzer

Kaley Harper knew in the tenth grade that God wanted her to teach other women about him. She discerned this life-long calling because of early faith and maturity resulting from a childhood illness that doctors could not diagnose. She remembers lying alone in a hospital bed repeating a verse her grandmother taught her: *When I am afraid, I will trust in you (Ps. 56:3).*

Now a bright and healthy twenty-something, Kaley looks back on her health challenges as the time when God captured her heart. She remembers, "I knew God was the one who made me, and he would be the one who had to fix me. I learned my life and body are not my own, and God will do with me as he wants."

She attended Dallas Theological Seminary to prepare for her calling, graduating in 2016 with a dual Master's in Christian Education and Biblical Studies. From counseling to theology, Kaley took a wide variety of classes to fully equip herself for ministry. She thrived in the seminary and was named both top female teacher and top Christian Education student in her graduating class.

When Kaley entered DTS, she assumed she would teach youth after graduation and eventually transition to being a women's minister at a church. However, God shifted her direction when a friend from Children's Relief International (CRI) asked her to lead a conference for pastors' wives in South Asia. Kaley initially refused because she feared the food, heat, and unknown. But she heard God whisper, "Do you not trust me to protect you and provide? There are women who desire to know me, and they're waiting for someone to come."

Kaley obeyed God's lead and flew to South Asia, where her conference was such a success that CRI offered to create a new role for her as an international women's ministry developer. Even though fears about working as a missionary overwhelmed Kaley and her family, she knew God wanted her to take the job. She realized, "As a single, I'm in a position to follow God anywhere and do whatever he wants. Why not say yes to him?"

At CRI, she has created the organization's Strength and Dignity Women's Ministry. She partners with national CRI leaders in South Asia, Mozambique, Myanmar, and Haiti to serve women in deep poverty. She writes cross-cultural curriculum that speaks to women with various educational levels and leads conferences to train them in Scripture. She also enables American women to use their talents for God as she recruits and trains teams to teach alongside her at conferences.

The women Kaley serves overseas remind her of Proverbs 31. She shared, "We can look at women in poverty and highlight their brokenness, but God has clothed them with strength and dignity (Prov. 31:25). They encourage me because they're on the front lines bringing their neighbors to God. They face persecution both physically and emotionally—and they're facing it well."

Kaley has encountered challenges in missions, such as battling spiritual warfare and navigating a transient life of going back and forth between her home base of Dallas and CRI's international sites. However, through it all, she beams, "My cup overflows. The most exciting thing ever is to be used by God doing exactly what he has designed you to do!"

CHAPTER 17

PARTNER WITH NATIONALS

Did you observe that in Russia and Rwanda we were invited by nationals? Our seminaries, colleges, and companies are full of men and women from other countries. Seek them out and learn from them. God may connect you with a Christian national who wants to minister back home and needs your resources. If you work together, you both will benefit and so will the kingdom of God.

Benefits of Working with Nationals

Cultural

Your friend has connections that will take you years to develop. She knows the language and is already accepted and trusted by her peers. She is culturally adjusted and understands the political climate.

Financial

It's more cost-effective. What does it cost to support a national's ministry in a developing country? About $50 to $100 a month! Most nationals will work in ministry an average of twenty-two years. You have invested between $132,000 and $264,000 for twenty-two years' work!

What does it cost to support an American overseas? On the average, $5,500 a month.[38] That's about $790,000—but that's just the total for twelve years, the average length of an American missionary's career. Two of those years are spent raising support and two years on furlough. That leaves eight years for ministry, including language training.

You do the numbers! Even if we invest $30,000 to put a national through seminary, we're still light years ahead. Even better than bankrolling nationals at an American seminary, send them to seminary in their own country. The cost is less and they are more likely to go home—those who study in the US sometimes don't.

The World Is Smaller

World conditions are conducive to partnering with nationals. We live in a communications/information-based world—sharing information online in moments. Ease of travel makes it practical. You can fly anywhere in the world in twenty-four hours.

Access

Nationals can go where we cannot go and are accepted in ways we will never be accepted. In addition, they continue to serve God long after Americans go home.[39]

They Need Our Resources

They know their own people's needs and they know how to reach them. But in two-thirds of the world, church communities need Western money and technology. When we traveled to Rwanda, not only did we pay our own passage, but we raised $10,000 to bring the Rwandan women leaders to the capital city. They didn't have enough to feed their children. Certainly they could not afford to travel to the capital. But women in our church sponsored Rwandan women with small donations of $10 and $15, and soon we raised the money to bring them all.

Can you think of a better investment? I remember the faces of the Rwandan women as we handed out Bibles in their own language. Afterward they danced and sang with glee.

It's Just Plain Practical

Partnering with nationals is productive. Most leaders believe that empowering nationals is more effective in promoting Christianity (86 percent) than is sending missionaries to other countries (12 percent).[40] You jumpstart your vision and accomplish far more long-term. Does this mean American missionaries no longer need to live overseas? Of course not. But we need to send them into places to do the tasks that nationals don't have the resources to do.

On the Russia project, Liz Loeffler lived in Moscow, returning to Dallas when necessary. She was vital to planning and communication between the team members here and there. Melody Wilson, a law school graduate turned missionary, based herself in Moscow for a while but traveled to visit and undergird the women's ministry regional training centers throughout Russia. Her skills and support were indispensable.

PARTNER WITH NATIONAL CHURCHES

"What's amazing is watching the nationals do missions themselves," says Lyndsay Murray, a woman who spent a year as a foreign exchange student in Moscow. She also invested time in her church's sister church in Penza, Russia—and the Penza Russians birthed missions in Murmansk, a region of 300,000 people within the Arctic Circle. Lyndsay's church and the nationals sent combined teams to Murmansk—a truly cross-cultural experience for all involved and a great witness to the people there that Christ can break down any walls that separate us.

Patrick Johnstone writes in *The Church Is Bigger Than You Think:*

> What is advocated is a partnership in servanthood each to the other so that the Church becomes what God always intended—a perfect Bride for His Son to co-reign with Him through all eternity. We have fallen far short of that ideal, therefore every effort must be made to repair broken bridges of understanding and fellowship and establish practical working relationships at every level so that we, the Church, might be one in love, the power of the Holy Spirit and vision for a lost world.[41]

What better way than to partner in missions with national churches.

Camino Global has invested over 125 years in Central America. Now it supports Latin American nationals as missionaries to the Middle East. In places where Americans cannot go due to political prejudice, these Latin Americans are accepted and more productive.

Missions today is in a time of transition. Americans partner with nationals to provide resources—people and money—and the people serve short- or long-term, depending on the needs. We must always ask "Where?" and "Why?"

before moving ahead. Accountability and impact are evaluated constantly to make good use of the gifts God has given. As the planet grows smaller, we can reach more of it for Christ—if we use new methods and mind-sets.

MINISTER THEIR WAY!

When I (Sue) was a child, we lived in Rhodes, a Greek island in the Aegean Sea. My father was a Coast Guard officer. One weekend as we drove through the tiny villages, my mother pointed out mammoth masses of metal rusting in the fields. "American missionaries brought tractors to help farmers," she explained, "but left them behind when the peasant farmers refused to adopt American farming methods. Now they sit rusting in the fields, without parts, as a reminder of American arrogance."

Dancing with Elephants!

Our best intentions can do damage! Listen to a story Africans tell about Americans:

> Elephant and Mouse were best friends. One day Elephant said, "Mouse, let's have a party!" Animals gathered from far and near.
>
> They ate. They drank. And nobody celebrated more and danced harder than Elephant. After the party was over, Elephant exclaimed, "Mouse, did you ever go to a better party? What a blast!" But Mouse did not answer.
>
> "Mouse, where are you?" Elephant called. He looked around for his friend, and then shrank back in horror. There at Elephant's feet lay Mouse. His little body was ground into the dirt. He had been smashed by the big feet of his exuberant friend, Elephant.

"Sometimes that is what it is like to do missions with you Americans," the African storyteller commented. "It is like dancing with an elephant."[42]

In our enthusiasm, we Americans often arrive as "fixers" and "rescuers." We bring our technology and money, assuming nationals will submit to our methods and ideas as a result. When we encounter resistance, we are wounded and return home feeling like unappreciated parents. Often we never understand that we have disrespected a culture. In our hurry to achieve our goals, we forget to honor timetables, learn courtesy from another per-spective, and develop relationships. We never mean to hurt anyone but, in our excitement, we can do more harm than good.

Do no harm—better yet, do great good! How do we dance with Mouse without harming her? How do we empower Mouse so that she directs the dance?

EXAMINE YOUR MOTIVES

Short-term missions is not a way to get other people to pay for your summer vacation. Long-term missions is not a way to escape problems at home. We don't go because we need to appreciate our blessings. We don't go to expose our youth to suffering. We don't go to expand our minds or to embrace a global perspective.

We don't send church members so they will give more to our missions projects or because they need a bonding experience. These are byproducts of the experience, benefits for us, but they will never empower or sustain us in the midst of the work.

It's not about us—it's about them—and even more, about God! "Watch your motives," warns Kathy Appleton, a former pastor of missions. "Even the motive of loving others is the wrong motive. The real fuel is a love for Christ and a passion to see Him glorified." When you are knee deep in mud, throwing up in a dirty bucket, or reworking your lesson for the third time, that's the motivation that keeps you going.

SELECT YOUR TEAM CAREFULLY

Who should minister cross-culturally? Who should lead your team?

Missions is not for sissies. If your idea of roughing it is slow room ser-vice, you're not ready. Ministering in another culture requires maturity, humility, and flexibility. The latter quality is so important, we'll devote an entire section to it.

On the other hand, missions is a great place to learn to live Philippians 2:3, *Do nothing out of selfish ambition or vain conceit. Rather, in humility value others above yourselves.* Your team leaders need to be seasoned, your new recruits teachable.

Walking into another culture with a project is far different than attempt-ing the same ministry in your own territory. People there don't think like you, talk like you, or work like you. They may not like you because they've been exposed to obnoxious Americans. Before they will hear you or trust you, they insist you respect their culture and have their best interests at heart.

Much up-front work must be done before you begin the actual project. A team member with an attitude that says, "You'd better accept me the way I am" will sabotage your efforts.

A Russian Experience

On a mission trip to Penza, Russia, Mary Bodien learned how difficult it can be to adjust to another culture. Exhausted from the transcontinental flight, the team was driven from the plane to the Russian church, where the pastor explained the rules for ladies. They learned that only immodest women crossed their legs. "I couldn't concentrate on anything else in the service," confessed Mary, "I was so concerned I would cross my legs unconsciously." Select a team who can adjust to these kinds of demands with a positive attitude and a sense of humor.

An African Experience

Our flight to Rwanda took forty hours, and our bags were lost. They contained all our conference supplies as well as our personal effects. We had no clothes, toothpaste, deodorant, curling irons, medicine, or supplemental food—only those things in our carry-ons.

We disembarked the plane and were whisked to the conference center—an open building with a cement floor. I (Sue) collapsed on a cot in our quarters with a full-blown migraine. The women had been waiting for us for two days, so Jackie and Alice left to teach the first session. I slept hard—my first rest in three days. I awoke suddenly, my migraine waning, to two discouraged women.

Exhausted and with no time to prepare, Alice had done her best to teach the first session. But children cried, women fidgeted, and about halfway through, a quarter of them stood up and walked out. Alice and Jackie had no idea why. They returned, looking to me for direction.

We prayed for God to help us understand and be overcomers. Then we processed what was happening. As I listened, suddenly I understood. Hundreds of women back home were praying for us. With all this prayer, these hindrances had to be part of God's plan. We discussed ways God might be allowing these struggles to promote his purposes. We learned that many of our students had traveled as long as we had, walking or riding a bus. They were exhausted too. We realized that our stylish clothes sitting in an airport in Belgium might be a hindrance to the women we were teaching. They had one change of clothes and now, so did we.

The hygiene in Africa makes close contact harder for Americans, but without deodorant, we realized it wouldn't be a hindrance much longer. All that had happened over the past three days would help us bond and understand the Rwandan women. We prayed again.

The next morning we learned that our students were from varied denominations and two tribes that had massacred each other. They gathered in groups by tribes, refusing to interact with those who had murdered their loved ones. Our first message that morning was on forgiveness, and we mixed them in small groups for discussion. Walls began to break down that morning—and by the last day the women were dancing and singing together.

We also learned that many of the women rode three hours each way on the bus every day to attend. And the bus left at 4:00—about midway into Alice's message the first afternoon.

We had turned to the Lord in our crisis and he answered. Find team members who have enough experience with the Lord to know what to do in a crisis. Find team members who have learned to depend completely on the Lord. Find humble servants who know that *only* by abiding in Christ can they accomplish anything. Cross-cultural ministry means that you are out of control. That's when the adventure begins.

PREPARE THOROUGHLY

How do you get ready? Learn about the culture. Find out about the women you are serving. Talk to nationals visiting America first. Meet and pray as a team as you strategize and plan together. Enlist others to pray for you.

One missions pastor binds a "prayer passport" booklet to hand out to the whole church. It contains pictures, goals, and prayer requests of everyone going on a mission trip for that season.

When I (Sue) joined the Russian faculty, we prepared by reading *Introduction to the Russian Soul.* We gathered monthly and then weekly before we left. We shopped for long skirts and scarves to cover our heads to teach. I left my diamond wedding ring at home and purchased a tiny gold band at a discount store. Makeup was limited to soft colors and nail polish stayed at home. Small jewelry was permissible but nothing flashy. All these adornments were obstacles to the Russian women, and we wanted to connect quickly. It was simply a matter of respect.

FLEX, FLEX, FLEX

Missions is messy. Toss the mental picture you have created because it won't go as planned. Unexpected situations will probably arise and you will need to adapt quickly and with a smile. Your preplanned schedule often won't work. In Rwanda, we worked late into the evening altering our lessons. Some students had college degrees, while others could not read and had never attended a class of any kind. We needed to adjust our material accordingly. In fact we only taught about half of what we prepared.

Expect the unexpected. Unusual living conditions. Strange food. A new language. Unreliable transportation. Different customs and dress. Worship styles and ceremony unlike anything you've experienced. The lights may go out. The toilets may not flush—if you have any. And you may be misunderstood. But if you bring a flexible attitude and a sense of humor, these inconveniences will simply be part of the experience—little things really when you consider the God you represent and the good he can do through you.

Ziplocs Come in Handy!

"Wake up! Wake up, Peggy! We must start for the airport now. It is 5 A.M. but a blizzard is raging and there is two feet of snow over the streets. We cannot get the car to the door of the apartment, so you will have to walk about four blocks to the wider street where the car can pick you up." Pavel's voice over the telephone was concerned but determined.

She knew he would get her to the Kiev airport for her flight home if anyone could. But with the blizzard it would take at least eight hours. Peggy Hanley had been in Ukraine for three weeks teaching women about "contentment." She would teach two days and then travel to the next class. Now she was tired and ready to go home, although her mind played back to last night's hugs and singing. Even though she was freezing as she walked the long four blocks, she felt an inner warmth that comes from a job well done.

Pavel and his friend were waiting in his 1962 black Ford that sat growling on the street.

The two jovial Ukrainians leaped out to embrace her with a kiss on each cheek and a hearty greeting.

"Sorry you had to walk. Car is cold and keep on dying. We must hurry now to make it to airplane."

They threw her luggage into the trunk as Peggy crawled into the backseat by herself.

Her skirt was soaking wet and she was thoroughly chilled. But soon the old heater kicked in and she could feel her feet. It was Sunday, and in Ukraine snowplows don't work on Sunday. So they followed the faint tracks of cars in front of them, sliding and praying.

Peggy battled motion sickness and in her travels took medicine for it every day. She had taken her usual dose, but with all the sliding she became violently nauseated. She popped another pill and then took something for the stomach upset caused by the first two pills for motion sickness. She settled in for the long trip.

Two hours later she felt that sensation when you know it won't be long until you need to stop. In Ukraine, no nice "Exxon" gas stations with a lovely sit down toilet exist. Occasionally along the highway you'll see an outhouse near a bus stop—but the nice green forest is usually more desirable.

Peggy verbalized her need to Pavel.

"I must stop. Can you find a place?"

Out into two feet of snow she waded again and returned with a very wet skirt.

As she trudged back up to the road, she realized that the car had died and Pavel was desperately trying to get it started again—with no success! Cars in Ukraine were often unreliable.

Peggy prayed, "Lord, make me content with whatever You have planned for today. Here in the forest for the day, in a strange farmhouse for the night, whatever."

Finally the car turned over and chugged.

"This car very bad when we stop. We cannot stop again," Pavel repeated over and over as they continued down the slippery road. Peggy knew they risked missing her plane or worse if they stopped again.

Four hours. That sensation returned again. Suddenly it dawned on her why. All three pills she had taken were diuretics. Oh, no!

Five hours and she was uncomfortable. Five and a half. She shifted her weight from side to side. She crossed her legs. She twiddled her fingers. *I'm going to have an accident. I've got to think of something.*

Seasoned travelers always pack ziploc bags. They come in handy to carry clothes, medicine, makeup, whatever—and she had several ziploc bags in her carry-on that sat by her feet. Quietly she unzipped the case and emptied the baggie. Fortunately she was wearing a skirt.

A moment later she rolled down the window—"for some fresh air"—and tossed the bag onto the shoulder of the road. Below-zero temperatures would soon freeze it. She chuckled as she pictured whoever found it in the spring.

Seven hours—and because of the diuretics, she used another baggie and tossed it out before they hit the city limits of Kiev. Two puzzled Ukrainians in the spring. No disrespect intended—there are times when a creative alternative is required, and this was one of them.

Peggy said, "The two guys who took me to the airport still tell this war story as the worst blizzard they have ever traveled in. I tell it differently. Amazingly, I did have the peace of contentment, the lesson I came to teach—not because I could do that—but because God gave it to me when I asked for it."

Bomb Scares and Bad Plumbing

When I (Sue) was in Moscow, teaching for the Russia project, we had a bomb scare. Police came to escort us out of the rooms. Actually no bomb existed. The government planned an election in the room where we met the next day, and they wanted us out so their German shepherds could sniff for bombs. But we didn't know that.

During another training session, the women stayed in a different hotel to save money. However, the heat and hot water didn't work and the showers barely trickled. But who wanted a shower with cold water and no heat anyway? The American team "sucked it up" and finished their mission without complaining (much). They tasted what Russian women face every day and returned home with greater compassion for their sisters and an enhanced appreciation of heat, hot water, and showers.

What would you have done in Peggy's or Sue's situation? Can you face these kinds of challenges with an attitude of adventure and a sense of humor? Remember: flexibility is not optional in cross-cultural ministry. Flex, flex, flex.

GIVE YOUR HOST WINGS

Conflict erupted during our Moscow trip. Each training session we provided our twenty-one students with a textbook—usually an American best-seller translated into Russian. The students wanted to copy the books and give them out to women in their churches. As they taught others, these books would be helpful. But copyright laws came into question.

In addition, Liz, the American anchor living in Moscow, objected. She wanted the women to learn to write their own material. Several of us felt her response was unrealistic and harsh. Why should they write their own books when we had already written them? I see now that she was right.

Don't give a man a fish—teach a man to fish! It's an old saying, but a good one for cross-cultural ministry. How do you prepare your host to go on without you? How do you empower her so that she picks up the baton? That's the long-term goal.

Wear her ministry shoes. What resources are available after you leave? Use them. Will she be using faxes, e-mail, the Internet, or a word processor? If not, don't use them either. Use her tools. What's her budget? Work within those parameters.

God gifts his children all over the world. Identify and equip women who can create needed curriculum and materials. One day your church may not send teams there. Or one day the borders may close to Americans. Begin now to prepare your host to stand on her own.

As you can see, we don't sugarcoat missions. It is challenging, but it is also rewarding if you go for God's glory and prepare yourself well. Doors to women's ministry are opening across the globe beckoning to everyday women like you and me. The Transformation Model is adaptable in any culture. If God is moving you toward the mission field, take these principles and get going.

How Do I Prepare Myself for Full-Time Missions?

Do you believe God wants you to minister cross-culturally as your life work? If so, you can choose from a variety of options. What do you want to do? Do you want to serve overseas? Are you ready to launch? If so, here's a suggested method to discern God's call and prepare.

Begin at Home!

Why go thousands of miles when another culture lives in your city? Immigrants from all over the world live in pockets of most major cities, transforming that area into a piece of their country. You'll find people who speak another language, order their lives by different customs, and often live in poverty.

Why not taste cross-cultural ministry there first? You may find your calling in the inner city. Certainly you will learn more about yourself.

> A journey of ten thousand miles may begin on a local bus. This is not glamorous. We may prefer *Afganistanitis,* that is, serving exotic people in exotic places. How much more exciting (and how much more under our control) that overseas trip may be than befriending Mexicans across town. After all, who knows but what they might show up on our doorstep for an exchange visit!
>
> Yet when these local Mexicans or Afghans or Vietnamese commend us to their families in their distant homelands, we will be welcomed there for long-term mission rooted in relationships.
>
> In any case, what benefits us, or our grandchildren, is not the top priority. Mission is not therapy. Christ did not come primarily to enhance his own experience. He came to serve, and he started with what was near at hand.[43]

I (Sue) cut my teeth on inner-city ministry years before I ministered overseas. My husband and I traveled regularly to South Dallas to *Voice of Hope.* Kathy Dudley founded the ministry and developed a thriving program for youth, their families, and the elderly. In time she turned the ministry over to black leaders who emerged from within the ministry. My husband tutored in the after-school program. We attended conferences on racial reconciliation and participated in programs where we worked side by side with other races. We ministered in prisons and incarcerated youth camps.

Try your hand at home first. Many of the skills and qualities you'll need overseas can be learned right here. In addition, the needs are overwhelming and just as important to God. You may find that you are a missionary to your own back yard.

THE CANDIDATING PROCESS

If you still believe God is calling you overseas, take a year or two and work through these three stages of candidate preparation.

> *If you have run with footmen and they have tired you out, Then how can you compete with horses?* (Jer. 12:5a NASB)

Stage One: Candidate

A candidate is an individual seriously considering the possibility of serving in career ministry. At this stage, ask God to show you how to best prepare yourself if God leads you into missions work. Connect with the missions pastor of your church and ask for guidance.

Take a missions class at a college or seminary. Read *Let the Nations Be Glad* by John Piper and other recommended books. Take an evangelism/ discipleship course. Do a gifts and aptitude assessment. Write your personal testimony.

Strengthen your intimacy with God. Read *The Pursuit of God* by A. W. Tozer or *Knowing God* by J. I. Packer. Practice the disciplines of Bible study and prayer.

Become involved in an accountability group in your church. Ask your group to pray for your decision and involve them in the process. Participate in a short-term mission trip and initiate a friendship with an international student or worker.

Examine your family relationships. Meet at least once with a counselor or staff member to evaluate the health of your relationship with parents, spouse, and children. Consider what this move might mean to loved ones. How are they feeling about the ministry?

Research mission agencies. Begin to seek God's guidance for a team of sending partners. At the end of a year, if God has given you a firm heart commitment to pursue full-time ministry overseas, proceed to stage two.

Stage Two: Apprentice

An apprentice is an individual who is committed to entering career ministry and is actively taking steps toward investigating the type of ministry/agency organization that she hopes will send her. She has crossed the line from "I'm willing to go, but planning to stay" to "I'm planning to go, but willing to stay."

Pray to discern the will of God. Research options for full-time ministry. Now it is time to learn all you can. Read Hudson Taylor's *Spiritual Secret, Shadow of the Almighty* by Elisabeth Elliot, and *Peace Child* by Don Richardson.

Recruit twenty-five prayer partners and take on a leadership role in your church for at least six months. Become a small group leader, Sunday school teacher, or youth sponsor. Plan and lead a short-term mission trip. Meet with missionaries on furlough.

Determine the target area, target ministry, and sending agency. Meet with them and work through their requirements. Cultivate relationships with their leaders and ask God to show you the best fit. Then meet with the pastor or elders of your church and ask for their blessing. Is God giving you a green light? Has he sent up any red flags? If not, proceed to stage three.

Stage Three: Appointee

An appointee has completed the necessary requirements and has been accepted by a sending agency. What's left to do?

Now is the time to complete an in-depth study of your target area and type of ministry. See your doctor for physicals and discuss any health concerns. Set your house in order.

It's also time to raise support. Ask for help from someone with experience. Many missionaries dislike asking for help. Some even turn a deaf ear to God as a result. Don't. Remember: God commands that we all invest in his work. You are providing others an opportunity to use their resources for eternity. God always provides for those he sends.

As your departure approaches, arrange with the church to commission you. Then depart for the field with joy and get ready for adventure. Nothing satisfies like glorifying God according to your design and gifts. As you have submitted to this process, you can be fairly sure you are where God wants you. And you'll be leaving the elephant at home.

APPENDIX A

SAMPLE JOB DESCRIPTIONS

Pastor to Women

Purpose of Position:
To train women to meet the needs of women, their families, and community through solid Bible teaching
To oversee the women's staff, board, and ministries

Reports to:
Executive Pastor

Relates Closely with:
Pastor to Men
Community Life Pastor
Children's Pastor
Community Care Pastor

Responsible for:
Women's Ministry Assistant
Interns

Position Objectives:
Execute the purpose of the church
- Recruit, equip, and oversee women's lead team
- Oversee the development of new ministries
- Oversee the development of women's ministry staff
- Cast vision for women's ministry

- Provide leadership in developing a long-term plan
- Develop a team of solid Bible teachers
- Dream big for the sake of the kingdom

Primary Gifts/Strengths:
Heart for God, seminary education, solid Bible training, excels in art of teaching, encompassing leader, team player, teacher/visionary

Bible Study Coordinator (Volunteer)

Reporting Relationship:
Women's Pastor

Primary Function:
To oversee the Bible study
To select and support a team of leaders to carry out details

Responsibilities:
- To serve as administrator of the class
- To call an assistant, with the Women's Pastor's approval, and train her to take over the class
- To select, call, and encourage both an administrative team and a small group leaders team
- To assist the Women's Pastor with leaders' meetings and to oversee the business agenda
- To coordinate and partner with other board members helping with the class (Music, Children, Affirmation)
- To oversee "kick off," "end of semester" events, or any other special programs relating to the Bible study
- To serve as the emcee of the Bible study, responsible for opening prayer and announcements
- To attend lead team meetings
- To attend lead team training
- To support Women's Ministry activities and other lead team members

APPENDIX B

SAMPLE BIBLE STUDY LESSON

Taken from *James: Discovering God's Delight in a Lived-Out Faith*,
The Discover Together Bible Study Series, by Sue Edwards
https://www.discovertogetherseries.com

Take an Honest Look in the Mirror

 Get Up and Go Follow-Up

In Lesson 2, you analyzed your response to a particular temptation. I asked you to name the sin you were fighting, to identify when you noticed you were tempted, and to consider these questions: What was your initial response and how did the sin entice you? Did you let it go a step further and take root in you? What did that look like and feel like at first and then later? Did you feel guilty or sad for giving in? How might you take James's counsel to heart and make a different decision next time? Since we all experience temptations regularly, consider sharing any insight gleaned so we can learn from one another.

Every day we look in the mirror to clean up and make up. What if we glanced in the mirror right after waking up and saw disheveled hair and not-so-fresh teeth but we never combed our hair or brushed our teeth? We care too much about our outer self to do that—but what about our inner self? What mirror do we look into to gauge if we are healthy and attractive inside? That's more important to God, to others, and ultimately to ourselves. In this lesson, James dares us to take a look in our inner-beauty mirror and respond to what we see.

So far, James has taught us how to think about our trials and how to navigate through them to strengthen our faith, our character, and our witness. In the rest of his letter, he deals with specific trials and temptations. He says, "True growth looks like this."

Topics include how we use words, deal with anger, pursue a pure life, exhibit compassion for the needy, love all people well, demonstrate authentic faith, live as a peacemaker, resist loving money, develop patience and perseverance, and practice prayer. The majority of our trials and temptations involve these critical areas of life. Just imagine if we mastered these challenges. We would discover the joy of living out our faith and would glorify God in the process. What a dazzling beauty we would be—inside, that is! That would actually make us more beautiful on the outside too. But we need God's help, and he provides that help through the rest of James's letter.

 Read James 1:19–21.

1. In verse 19, James issues three commands. List them. What part of the human body does each involve?

A.

B.

C.

2. Imagine you are in a difficult conversation with a friend, co-worker, or family member over an issue that's important to you both. How might complying with the first two commands impact the third? If you fail to follow James's advice, what might easily result (1:20)?

3. Can you recall a time when you were slow to listen, quick to speak, and quick to become angry and these responses did not "produce the righteousness that God desires"? If you are comfortable, share what you learned so others can benefit from your experience and thus redeem it.

4. Which of James's three commands do you struggle with most? Any idea why? (Stay tuned—James offers us detailed help on these three disciplines later in his letter.)

5. In verse 21, James reveals two actions to help us gain victory in our trials and temptations—one negative and one positive. What are they?

Get rid of _____

Accept _____

6. Our culture brims with "moral filth" and "evil" today. Name as many examples as you can. Which encroach on your life?

7. We are instructed to influence the world for Christ but not to let the world pollute us. We must be involved in the world yet somehow stay untarnished by it. What insight can you offer to help us navigate this tension?

8. What do you need to purge from your life to help you overcome trials and temptations?

9. James exhorts us to "humbly accept the word planted in you" (1:21). Dissect these words.

What is "the word"?

What is James assuming? How can you accept something you don't know?

What do you think he means when uses the words *humbly* and *planted*?

What heart-attitude is he requesting?

10. Why is discovering the joy of living out your faith impossible if you fail to comply with the two mandates in verse 21?

Verse 21 ends with a result clause, "which can save you." Some have mistakenly assumed this refers to being saved from eternal damnation. However, the word *save* is used several different ways in the Bible. Sometimes it means trusting in the sacrifice of Jesus on the cross for eternal life. Other times it means healed from disease or saved from destruction in battle. Still other times it means saved from the consequences of our sin or saved from experiencing a miserable life or even premature death brought on by our sins. We draw the author's meaning from the context. In his letter, James writes about how to discover joy by living out our faith. In context then, verse 21 means that following his instructions can save us from a miserable life due to consequences of our own sin and foolish choices.

Thomas Constable explains further:

> Some interpreters have understood the phrase "which is able to save your souls" to imply that the souls of James's readers still needed to experience salvation from eternal damnation. However, since his readers were Christians (vv. 1–2), some interpreters believe that when a believer sins he loses his salvation and needs saving again. Yet the words James used, and their context, make it clear that this was not what he meant. . . . By obeying God's Word, the believer can save (preserve) his "life," himself (i.e., his entire self: body, soul, and spirit) from the consequences of sin. The ultimate consequence of sin for a believer is premature physical (not eternal) death (cf. 1:15; 5:19–20; Prov. 10:27; 11:19; 12:28; 13:14; 19:16; Rom. 8:13; 1 Cor. 11:30; 1 John 5:16). (*Notes on James*, 24)

 Read James 1:22–25.

11. Verse 22 sums up the main message of the whole book. What is the theme verse and what does it tell you?

12. Have you observed a Christian who knows God's Word well but fails to put it into practice? Why is this so dangerous for themselves, for others around them, and for God's reputation?

13. James paints a picture of people like that in verses 23 and 24. What are they like?

14. What might cause someone to hear God's Word but quickly walk away and forget it?

15. In contrast, describe the Christian in verse 25. How might this apply to how we deal with trials and temptations? What can this believer expect as a result?

16. What do you think James means by the phrase "the perfect law that gives freedom"? James is not talking about the Mosaic law in the Old Testament. How do the following passages help?

Matthew 22:36–40

James 2:8

Galatians 2:19–20

Galatians 3:1–5

17. James wraps up this section of his letter by providing a mirror for us to see what true spiritual maturity looks like (1:26–27). What three areas of our Christian life does he ask us to evaluate?

A.

B.

C.

18. If we walk away from this mirror and ignore what it shows us, who are we deceiving? In what sense is our religion "worthless"?

James's letter is strong, blunt, and convicting. How are you feeling toward James and his letter right now? Remember that almighty God who speaks through James has your best interests at heart. If your response is guilt or shame, repent, but don't become disheartened. Discouragement is the enemy's way of tempting you to get so down on yourself that you deny, neglect, distract yourself, or ultimately give up. Your heavenly Father loves you unconditionally and he wants to help you grow and thrive. Cooperate with him and be transformed.

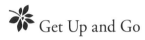 ## Get Up and Go

James describes three actions that we can use to measure whether or not we are growing up in Christ: how we use our tongues, whether we help the legitimately needy, and whether or not we pursue a pure life.

As we each look into our inner-beauty mirror, we could easily feel overwhelmed with guilt, realizing we don't measure up. Typically, our response might be to create a self-help plan composed of formulaic steps to alleviate the guilt or shame we feel. That's a natural reaction, but it doesn't work! Your self-help plan will likely fall the way of millions of New Year's resolutions—quickly forgotten, adding more guilt or shame. So what do we do?

We draw close to God and ask him to guide us, empower us, and work through us. We talk to him about all the ways we don't measure up. We acknowledge we are helpless without him, and we determine to cooperate with the Holy Spirit as he shows us the way.

How do we begin? Our activity this week is to set aside time to ask God to show you where he wants you to focus, related to the three crucial areas of your Christian life—your tongue, helping others, and purity. Eliminate and concentrate. You'll have time for the others later.

What time works best for you? Where could you get away from the bustle of daily life and simply rest in him?

As you go about your day, pay attention to any related inner promptings as well as experiences or situations you encounter. Ask God to provide clarity and wisdom. Remember in Lesson 2 that God promised to give us the wisdom we need but warned us against being a "drifting double-minded doubter." If you struggle with doubt, ask God to help you trust him. Inner beauty is a byproduct of your relationship with God.

APPENDIX C

TRAINING GUIDE FOR SMALL GROUP LEADERS

Studying God's Word together is an exciting adventure, requiring a leader. Thank you for your willingness to lead the group. Your role as leader is to guide a discussion characterized by

- A nonthreatening climate conducive to an honest exchange of ideas;
- A flow of stimulating and meaningful interaction;
- The presentation of God-honoring, biblically based insight.

What can you do to help the group succeed?

1. PUT THE WOMEN AT EASE

Express care for the women from the moment the first woman walks in the door until the last woman leaves. Greet them as they arrive. Initiate conversation before the discussion begins. Draw out women by asking nonthreatening questions such as "How long have you lived here?" or "Tell me a little about yourself." Especially focus on the woman who seems shy or lonely. Provide name tags to help women learn each other's names. Set an atmosphere of unconditional love and inclusion where women can relax, learn, and share.

- *Be other-centered!* This is not the time to visit with your best friend. You are your group's shepherdess! Many women are in

255

dreary circumstances and have varied spiritual needs. Make walking into your group a highlight of their week!

- *Develop good listening skills.* By intentional, focused listening, you convey that the participation of each group member is valued.

You may be the only reflection of Christ some women ever see!

2. BEGIN AND END ON TIME

Get started on time even if only two or three are there. Late arrivals will soon learn they must be prompt. There will always be stragglers. Begin without them. Quickly and graciously greet them when they arrive. And honor women's busy lives by ending when you said you would, but allow women who want more fellowship to remain behind and enjoy visiting.

3. BEGIN WITH ENTHUSIASM

Ask someone who is enthusiastic to answer the first question. Get off to an exciting start! Keep your eyes off your study guide as much as possible. Look at the women as they are speaking. Train yourself not to just read aloud lesson notes or the introductory paragraph, but instead rephrase it and speak it out in your own words.

4. ASSUME AUTHORITY (BUT REMAIN GRACIOUS)

- Be firm but not bossy.
- Be gentle but stay in control.

Someone has to be in charge, and you are it! The women expect you to lead. If you are naturally soft-spoken, make a deliberate effort to project your voice. Sit up and direct the group. You are there to keep the group on target and make sure time is not wasted. This is a serious role but don't forget to maintain your sense of humor and have fun.

5. Encourage *Discussion*

The discussion group leader is *not* a lecturer. *After* the discussion, you may want to wrap up the study with a formal lecture, but during the discussion the leader does not teach. She does not spotlight herself as the one with the answers but instead focuses on the women in the group. Her role is

- To direct the flow of the discussion;
- To encourage interaction;
- To set the climate or tone;
- To guard against poor use of time;
- To lead the group in an understanding of the material.

Establish an atmosphere of unconditional acceptance where each member is free to share what she's thinking and feeling. We may not always agree with a woman's view, but we can respect her by listening thoughtfully to her ideas.

As a leader you do not correct or "straighten out" women in the group. Avoid saying "No," or "But . . ." Some possible responses when you hear an unusual answer are

- "I've never thought of it in that way."
- "That's an interesting perspective."
- "I see what you're saying."

We want an atmosphere where each woman shares what the Holy Spirit is teaching her through God's Word. Women need to feel they can ask their questions and not be made to feel foolish.

It is imperative, though, that a biblical perspective be presented. Draw out women who have solid biblical insight to present their views when the group needs to hear a biblical answer. In this way, women hear the biblical perspective, but no one in the group is singled out as the one with the wrong answer. As women continue studying the Bible, they soon discover God's perspectives for themselves.

6. Consider Calling on Women by Name

This is better than asking for a volunteer to answer a question because

- Usually the same few women volunteer;
- Waiting for volunteers consumes time, causing discussions to drag.

This is also your greatest tool for maintaining control! You can bring out shy women while keeping talkers from dominating. Call on the quiet women early in the discussion because often when they have participated and been affirmed, they find it easier to speak up. If you prefer not to call on women by name, do your best to give everyone an opportunity to participate.

Move quickly through questions with obvious answers. For example, observation questions can be answered easily right from the text. Call on one person and then move on, or quickly answer the question yourself as a transition to other kinds of questions.

Spend most of the discussion time on sharing and opinion questions. Sharing and opinion questions bring out interesting discussion. Your ultimate goal is to encourage natural interaction. As the women become more comfortable, you'll see a more natural interchange, with women speaking up in response to one another. This makes the group less like a question-and-answer schoolroom session. That's good!

This type of discussion, however, takes more skill to control. If the group becomes chaotic and the quieter ones are not participating, step back in and take control. Otherwise, let this more natural interaction continue—but learn to sum up ideas expressed and move on to the next question when appropriate. You are responsible for the flow of discussion.

7. Use Volunteers for Share Questions

Let the women know that personal questions are for volunteers only! It's inappropriate to ask a woman to reveal personal information unless she's ready. Our goal, however, is to share our heartaches and struggles. How can you facilitate a deep level of personal sharing? Be ready to share on personal application questions occasionally. Be real with the group! A great benefit of discussion groups is that we build community when participants open up about their fears or feelings of inadequacy. Guard against spending too much time, though, working through personal problems. Life's answers are found in Scripture.

8. BE SURE EVERY COMMENT IS AFFIRMED!

The leader must be sure every comment is acknowledged in a positive way. Nothing feels more awkward than to express an idea and have it ignored. This conveys rejection. If no one else in the group interacts or responds to the comment, then the leader must affirm the group member with warm words like, "Thank you for your insight," or at least, "That's an interesting way of looking at it." Try to respond as you would in everyday conversation, as naturally as possible. *Affirming the women is a necessity!*

Quick affirmations besides "good point":

Excellent	Fantastic
Super	Great answer
Wonderful	Terrific
Wow	Fabulous
Absolutely	I agree
What insight	That was deep
I like that	Wish I'd thought of that

Some affirmations for the group are:

- "I'm so happy to see all of you!"
- "There are many places you could be today, and I'm so glad you chose to be here!"
- "Thank you for being so well prepared!"
- "I appreciate each one of you and the effort you made to be here."

9. KEEP UP THE PACE

The pace of the discussion is determined by the personalities of the group members and the skill and preparation of the leader. Observe the pace of your group. Is it peppy or does it drag? Develop strategies to keep the group moving and interesting. There are two extremes, and each requires a different response.

A. The Quiet Group

Does your group hesitate to answer? Do you feel like you are "pulling teeth" to get them to participate? Then you have a quiet group. They often water-ski over issues and are content with pat answers. Their pace is too slow—it drags—and they tend to finish quickly. But when the discussion is over, it wasn't very interesting. What can you do to perk up a quiet group and shoot it full of energy?

- Muster enthusiasm.
- Encourage, encourage, encourage.
- Be patient; intimacy takes time.
- Ask energetic women to interject stimulating questions to spark interest.
- Draw out answers by calling on many women for each question.
- Don't settle for a pat answer.

B. The Talkative Group

This group has difficulty finishing the questions because so many women want to participate. The pace is perky and fun, but the discussion is easily sidetracked. When you go down rabbit trails, you talk about issues unrelated to the Bible study. This is frustrating for women who want to understand and apply the passage. When you seldom finish the lesson, the more serious students become discouraged.

The group is filled with women who love to talk and have interesting ideas to contribute. The problem comes when the more verbal women dominate those who are less articulate and when the group can't get through the lesson. What can you do?

- Assume a greater air of authority.
- Privately elicit the more talkative women's help in drawing out quieter women.
- Cut off talkers (as graciously as possible).

To refocus a group, here are some things you could say:

- "In the interest of our time remaining, let's move on."
- "Let's pick up the pace a little."
- "Let's finish that discussion after Bible study."
- "Let's finish our questions, and then we'll come back to this."

Whenever the group is sidetracked, the leader must decide how much time she will spend there. Pursue a rabbit trail *briefly* if it is of common interest and time allows. Then get back to the meat of the lesson. Do your utmost to finish every week. The women expect it!

What should you do if a woman breaks down in tears? This *special circumstance* can stall the pace and tempt the group to get sidetracked for the rest of the lesson. *DON'T!*

Be sensitive but also think of the group as a whole. The group often wants to spend the remaining time consoling, counseling, and fixing the problem. You can't! Allow a couple minutes of tender feedback, but then step in and *pray briefly* for the woman. Assure her you will talk with her later. Then move on. Later, talk with her privately and give her your encouragement and support. But *do not discontinue working through the lesson.*

10. CONTROL YOUR OWN TALKING

The leader is in ministry to others. This is the participants' time! If the group is talkative, the leader should limit her talking. If the group tends to be quiet, talk to prime the pump and then back off when the women are participating.

11. MAINTAIN UNITY OF SPIRIT

Never speak in a critical manner about any church or denomination, and do your best to discourage this kind of talking in the group. Redirect the conversation. This kind of criticism is divisive, destroying the unity we're striving to build. A woman in the group may be offended if another group member slanders a group she grew up in or respects. Avoid politics.

12. STAY IN TOUCH WITH YOUR GROUP

Keep in touch regularly with your group—by voice, text, or email. If you never contact them, you are sending them a message that you don't care! Let them know that you are praying for them—especially if they are absent. This builds relationships. If a new member joins the group, be sure to call the first week to answer any questions and familiarize her with group procedures. You are a shepherdess—so tenderly nurture your flock.

WILL YOUR GROUP PRAY TOGETHER?

You need to decide if part of your group time will be spent praying for the specific needs of women in your group. If so, here are suggested methods:

- Let the women know that there will be prayer time and ask them to submit a *personal* request.
- Encourage the women to write out their requests as they do their lesson rather than waiting to do so after they arrive.
- Ask your group to write down their prayer requests on 3 x 5 index cards.
- Collect the cards and *you* (the leader) read the requests aloud to the group. Share any answered prayer at this time.
- Either pass the cards back out to the group or place them in the middle.
- Ask the group members each to pick a card and pray for the request during the group prayer time or during the week.
- As the leader is reading the requests, the women can write them down, or one person can keep a group prayer journal.
- A volunteer can e-mail the requests to group members.

APPENDIX D

CONFLICT RESOLUTION COVENANT

As a member of the Women's Ministry Board, I agree to follow the biblical pattern for resolving conflict in Matthew 18:15–17.

> If your sister sins against you, go and show her the fault, just between the two of you. If she listens to you, you have won your sister over. But if she will not listen, take one or two others along, so that every matter may be established by the testimony of two or three witnesses. If she still refuses to listen to them, tell it to the church; and if she refuses to listen even to the church, treat her as you would a pagan or a tax collector. (in feminine terms)

This means:

1. If I am offended and cannot overlook the offense (Prov. 17:9; 19:11), I will contain the conflict by "going and showing her the fault, just between the two of us." If I need counsel, I will consult the Women's Pastor or Director of Women's Ministries. I agree not to involve other parties as this can lead to factions (2 Cor. 12:20; Prov. 16:28; James 4:11a).

2. If the conflict is not resolved after I "go and show," I will work to resolve the conflict with the Women's Pastor and Director of Women's Ministries, the other party, and any "witnesses" who might help resolve the differences in a gracious and godly manner. I agree not to

discuss this matter with those who are not directly involved.

3.   If the conflict is still not resolved, I can "tell it to the church." How-
     ever, I will not go to "the church" without informing the Women's
     Pastor and Director of Women's Ministries as well as the other party.
     If I meet with "the church," I agree to invite the other party and
     women's ministry leadership to go with me so that we can all be
     heard at the same time.

Name: _____ **Date:** _____

APPENDIX E

WOMEN STUDENT FELLOWSHIP CONSTITUTION

Article I—NAME
The name of this organization shall be "ARISE of Dallas Theological Seminary." For publicity, the name may be reflected as "DTS ARISE" or "ARISE Women Student Fellowship."

Article II—PURPOSE
The purpose of ARISE is to provide opportunities for connection, engagement, and encouragement within the body of women students at the Dallas campus. This includes providing events and activities to help women students prepare for ministry in whatever area God has called them, and to help acclimate new students to campus. We will accomplish this through regular gatherings which may include, but are not limited to, the following:

a) monthly #TrendingTopics forums or other guest speaker events
b) an annual Retreat
c) Lunch Connections or other social gatherings
d) New Student Luncheons
e) Other programs, events, activities, and gatherings as approved by the Board

Article III—PARTICIPATION AND MEMBERSHIP IN ARISE
Participation in ARISE is open to all women students at Dallas Theological Seminary. Membership is not required.

Article IV—STRUCTURE OF THE ARISE BOARD

Section 1. The ARISE Board (the "Board") is the governing body. The Board consists of current women students appointed by the current Board Members and the Faculty/Staff Advisor (the "Advisor"). An honorary and permanent position is given to the Advisor for Women Students at Dallas Theological Seminary as the Advisor.

Section 2. The Board and the Advisor shall report to the Dean of Students at Dallas Theological Seminary.

Section 3. The Board will consist of a minimum of 6 and a maximum of 15 members (the "Board Members").

Section 4. The minimum positions required for the Board to operate are: President, Vice President, Secretary, Retreat Chair, Hospitality, and Advisor.

Section 5. The Board President is appointed in the spring semester by the current Board President and the Advisor. This position will be filled by a woman student who has served on the Board. In the rare case that no one who has previously served on the Board can fill the President role for the subsequent year, an exception may be made with the express approval of the Advisor. This appointment will be announced by the March Board meeting.

Section 6. Board Members are recommended by the outgoing Board President and the incoming Board President, and then selected with the approval of the Advisor.

Section 7. Each Board Member must make a one academic-year commitment, which begins effective April 1 of the previous academic year and runs through summer, fall, winter, and spring semesters, then concluding in March of the academic year served.

Section 8. Board Members can serve multiple years on the Board, but cannot serve in the same position on the Board for more than two consecutive years.

Section 9. A Board Member may fill more than one position simultaneously.

Article V—MEETINGS AND ACTIVITIES OF THE BOARD

Section 1. The Board will meet together a minimum of seven times during the year in which they serve. Each Board Member must commit to attending a minimum of five of the Board meetings. Extenuating circumstances can be considered by the President or Advisor for approval prior to the absence.

Section 2. In the event that a Board Member is unable to complete their responsibilities to the Board, they shall meet with the President and Advisor to discuss the situation. If a Board Member is not fulfilling their responsibilities through a failure to attend the required number of meetings or not completing the duties of their position, the President and/or the Advisor may remove the Board Member from the Board and appoint a new student to the position after meeting with the Board Member to discuss the situation.

Section 3. Board meetings will generally be the second Tuesday of each month during the academic year from 11:30 a.m. –12:45 p.m. at a location on campus to be determined and communicated to the Board by the President. At the beginning of each academic year, a full schedule of Board meetings and activities will be distributed to all Board Members by the President.

Section 4. Other meetings shall be held as needed to help facilitate the purpose of the organization as stated in Article II above.

Section 5. The Board will meet at least seven times during the one-year term of service. A quorum for a valid Board meeting is 50 percent of Board Members in attendance.

Section 6. The Board will develop and hold an annual ARISE retreat (the "Annual Retreat") or similar activity for all current DTS women students.

Section 7. The Board will hold an annual retreat for incoming Board Members ("the "Board Retreat") each Spring Semester. Those attending will be the incoming Board Members and the Advisor. The outgoing Board Members may be invited to attend if there are activities for both Board Members established by the incoming President. The purpose of this Board Retreat will be to build rapport between the new Board members, as well as to cast vision, plan, and set the calendar for the upcoming academic year's events and activities.

Section 8. If the outgoing Board Members are not included in the Board Retreat, then the final Board meeting of the academic year for the outgoing Board will be used as a transition event to the incoming Board. The purpose of this meeting will be to recognize the outgoing Board Members, and to train the incoming Board Members for their new roles on the Board.

Article VI—AMENDMENTS AND BYLAWS
Any amendment of this constitution by change or addition to the Articles must receive a two-thirds majority vote of all Board Members. Proposed amendments must be distributed to all Board Members at least seven days in advance of the Board meeting at which discussion and voting on the amendment(s) are to take place.

ENDNOTES

Introduction

1. https://www.cbsnews.com/news/in-a-first-women-surpass-men-in-college-degrees/.
2. https://www.census.gov/newsroom/facts-for-features/2017/single-americans-week.html.
3. https://www.dol.gov/wb/stats/s.tats_data.htm.
4. See www.census.gov.

Chapter 1: Who Is the Postmodern Woman?

5. Personal correspondence with author Sue Edwards.
6. Personal correspondence to Sheldon Vanauken.
7. Dennis Sheridan, "Modern and Postmodern Challenges to Liberal Education," in *The Liberal Arts in Higher Education: Challenging Assumptions, Exploring Possibilities,* eds. Diana Glyer and David Weeks (Landham, MD: University Press of America, 1998), 41.
8. Len Sweet, *SoulTsunami: Sink or Swim in the New Millennium Culture* (Grand Rapids: Zondervan, 1999), 17.
9. Ibid., 27.
10. Ibid.
11. Ibid., 400.
12. Ibid., 78.
13. Ibid., 83–85.
14. See www.barna.org.
15. Ronald Mayers, "Apologetic to Postmodernism: General Revelation and the Fifth Gospel" (paper presented at the Annual Meeting of the Evangelical Theological Society, Orlando, FL, November 1998), 21.
16. Sweet, *SoulTsunami,* 385.
17. Ibid., 410.
18. https://www.barna.com/research/meet-spiritual-not-religious/.
19. http://www.pewresearch.org/fact-tank/2016/01/21/americans-spirituality/.

Chapter 2: What Is the Transformation Model?

20. Don Simmons, "Know Your Stuff, Know Who You're Stuffing, and Then Stuff It," *Explorer Lite* #37, May 21, 2001, www.leadnet.org.

Chapter 3: Begin Right!

21. *Washington Post,* 13 March 2001.
22. Vickie Kraft, *Women Mentoring Women* (Chicago: Moody, 1992), 47.
23. Ibid., 47–48.

Chapter 4: Build Your Team

24. *Washington Post,* 13 March 2001.

Chapter 5: Rally Your Team

25. George Cladis, *Leading the Team-Based Church* (San Francisco: Jossey-Bass, 1999), 1.
26. Ibid., 25.
27. Ibid., 139.
28. Ibid., 121.

Chapter 6: Create Your Own Life-Changing Bible Studies

29. Bruce Wilkinson, *Walk Thru the New Testament* (Atlanta: WTB, Inc., 1995), 4.
30. *Purpose* (Irving, TX: Wisdom Works Ministries) Issue 5 (September 1998).
31. George Cladis, *Leading the Team-Based Church* (San Francisco: Jossey-Bass, 1999), 21.
32. http://sarahbessey.com/in-which-i-write-letter-to-womens/.

Chapter 12: Prepare for and Survive Conflict

33. You may contact Peacemaker Ministries at mail@HisPeace.org or visit their website at www.HisPeace.org.

Chapter 13: Ministering with Men

34. Elizabeth Inrig, *Release Your Potential* (Chicago: Moody, 2001), 176.

Woman of Influence—Karen Swallow Prior

35. https://www.thegospelcoalition.org/blogs/trevin-wax/know-your-southern-baptists-karen-swallow-prior/.
36. https://thewell.intervarsity.org/in-focus/seamless-calling-karen-swallow-prior.

Chapter 16: Strategies That Work Worldwide

37. David Mays, personal correspondence with author Sue Edwards.

Chapter 17: Partner with Nationals

38. Numbers based on several resources, including Mission Network News www.mnnonline.org/news/understanding-the-cost-of-missionary-support/, www.imb.org, and www.goefca.org
39. Patrick Johnstone and Jason Mandryk, *Operation World* (Waynesboro, GA: Paternoster, 2001), 2.
40. http://www.pewforum.org/2011/06/22/global-survey-priorities/.
41. Patrick Johnstone, *The Church Is Bigger Than You Think* (Pasadena, CA: William Carey Library, 1998), 210.
42. Miriam Adeney, "Short Term Missions Today," in *When the Elephant Dances, the Mouse May Die* (Pasadena, CA: Bill Berry, 2000), 8.
43. Ibid., 11.

Organic
MENTORING

A MENTOR'S
GUIDE TO
RELATIONSHIPS
WITH NEXT
GENERATION
WOMEN

SUE EDWARDS & BARBARA NEUMANN

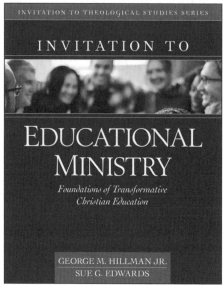

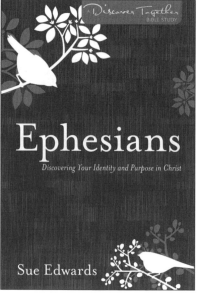